LOST BOY

Never Land Grows Up

Book and lyrics by Phil Willmott

Music by Mark Collins and Phil Willmott

samuelfrench.co.uk

ISBN 978-0-573-11516-5

www.samuelfrench.co.uk

www.samuelfrench.com

FOR AMATEUR PRODUCTION ENQUIRIES

UNITED KINGDOM AND WORLD
EXCLUDING NORTH AMERICA
plays@samuelfrench.co.uk
020 7255 4302/01

Each title is subject to availability from Samuel French, depending upon country of performance.

THINKING ABOUT PERFORMING A SHOW?

There are thousands of plays and musicals available to perform from Samuel French right now, and applying for a licence is easier and more affordable than you might think

From classic plays to brand new musicals, from monologues to epic dramas, there are shows for everyone.

Plays and musicals are protected by copyright law so if you want to perform them, the first thing you'll need is a licence. This simple process helps support the playwright by ensuring they get paid for their work, and means that you'll have the documents you need to stage the show in public.

Not all our shows are available to perform all the time, so it's important to check and apply for a licence before you start rehearsals or commit to doing the show.

LEARN MORE & FIND THOUSANDS OF SHOWS

Browse our full range of plays and musicals and find out more about how to license a show
www.samuelfrench.co.uk/perform

Talk to the friendly experts in our Licensing team for advice on choosing a show, and help with licensing
plays@samuelfrench.co.uk   020 7387 9373

 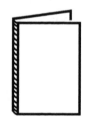

ABOUT THE AUTHOR
PHIL WILLMOTT

Multi-award-winning composer, writer and director Phil Willmott's first collaboration as a composer with Mark Collins was the musical *Lost Boy*, which transferred from the Finborough Theatre for an extended run at the Charing Cross Theatre and imagined the characters from *Peter Pan* as adults in the First World War. Following the success of *Lost Boy*, Mark and Phil have subsequently collaborated on *Princess Caraboo* (also published by Samuel French), which premiered to great critical acclaim at the Finborough Theatre in 2016 and completed commissions for Adam Kenwright and Shakespeare's Globe. Phil Willmott's first musical was a finalist for the prestigious Vivian Ellis Prize, and his subsequent, internationally published and regularly revived musicals include *Once Upon a Time at the Adelphi* (also published by Samuel French), commissioned by Liverpool Playhouse (TMA Award winner and WhatsOnStage nominee for Best Musical Production in the UK), and its US version *Once Upon a Time at the Atlantic City*, which premiered in Connecticut and won five Spirit of Broadway Awards, including Best Score and Best Direction; *Around the World in Eighty Days*, written for BAC and revived at Liverpool Playhouse, for a UK tour, and a two-year German tour; the *Dick Barton Special Agent* trilogy, originally commissioned by Croydon Warehouse and revived at Oldham Coliseum, Nottingham Playhouse, The Queen's Theatre in Hornchurch, Theatre by the Lake in Keswick, The Yvonne Arnaud Theatre in Guildford, Greenwich Theatre, New Wimbledon Theatre and at Southwold Rep; and adaptations of *Treasure Island* and *Jason and the Argonauts*, all of which continue to be licensed regularly by Samuel French across the globe. The adaptation of *Lysistrata* he wrote with Germaine Greer was recently presented as part of the Almeida's Greek Season starring Tamsien Grieg, and his adaptation of Gorky's *The Lower Depths* is published by Oberon Books. His recent plays in London include a dramatisation of Wagner's *Ring Cycle* which played to 40,000 people at the Scoop; *Captain Show-Off* adapted from the Roman Comedies of Plautus, and Euripides' Trojan War trilogy (also at the Scoop); *Play of Thrones*, a popular amalgamation of the Shakespeare that inspired George R. R. Martin (Union Theatre); *Encounter*, a new gay love story inspired by *Brief Encounter* (Above the Stage Theatre), and his reworking of Gilbert and Sullivan's *Princess Ida*, which played for a sell-out run at the Finborough Theatre in 2015. He often writes about musical theatre as a regular columnist for *The Stage* and reviews West End and Broadway musicals for toplondontheatre.com. His website is www.philwillmott.org

ABOUT THE COMPOSER

MARK COLLINS

Mark is a London based musical director, pianist and composer/
arranger. His theatre credits include *Dreamgirls* (Savoy Theatre),
Billy Elliot The Musical (Victoria Palace), *Wicked* (Apollo
Victoria), *Jersey Boys* (Prince Edward), *The Secret Diary of
Adrian Mole* (Leicester Curve), *Exposure* (St James) and
multiple workshops and productions of new writing both in
the UK and New York.

Productions at the Finborough Theatre include co-composer,
orchestrations and musical supervision for *Lost Boy* (which
subsequently transferred to Charing Cross Theatre) and *Princess
Caraboo*, musical supervisor for Adam Guettel's *Myths and
Hymns*, and musical director for Grant Olding's *Three Sides*.

www.markcollinsmd.co.uk

MUSIC USE NOTE

Licensees are solely responsible for obtaining formal written permission from copyright owners to use copyrighted music in the performance of this play and are strongly cautioned to do so. If no such permission is obtained by the licensee, then the licensee must use only original music that the licensee owns and controls. Licensees are solely responsible and liable for all music clearances and shall indemnify the copyright owners of the play(s) and their licensing agent, Samuel French, against any costs, expenses, losses and liabilities arising from the use of music by licensees. Please contact the appropriate music licensing authority in your territory for the rights to any incidental music.

USE OF COPYRIGHT MUSIC

A licence issued by Samuel French Ltd to perform this play does not include permission to use the incidental music specified in this copy.

Where the place of performance is already licensed by the PERFORMING RIGHT SOCIETY (PRS) a return of the music used must be made to them. If the place of performance is not so licensed then application should be made to the PRS, 2 Pancras Square, London, N1C 4AG.

A separate and additional licence from
PHONOGRAPHIC PERFORMANCE LTD,
1 Upper James Street, London W1F 9DE (www.ppluk.com)
is needed whenever commercial recordings are used.

IMPORTANT BILLING AND CREDIT REQUIREMENTS

If you have obtained performance rights to this title, please refer to your licensing agreement for important billing and credit requirements.

Lost Boy premiered at the Finborough Theatre Monday 13th January – Saturday, 15 February 2014. Produced by Neil McPherson and The Steam Industry. It subsequently transferred to the Charing Cross Theatre in the West End for an extended limited run presented by Steven M. Levy and The Steam Industry, in association with Neil McPherson for the Finborough Theatre.

CAPTAIN GEORGE LLEWELLYN DAVIES and PETER PAN	Steven Butler
LOST WIFE MABEL, LOST BOY TWIN 2 and DANCE CAPTAIN	Lauren Cocoracchio
WENDY DARLING	Grace Gardner
LOST WIFE LADY EDITH	Hannah Grace
LOST BOY CURLY and JOHN DARLING	Richard James-King
LOST WIFE CISSIE and TIGER LILLY	Natalie Lipin
LOST BOY NIBS	Luka Markus
TOOTLES	Max Panks
LOST BOY SLIGHTLY	David Scotland
LOST BOY TWIN 1 and MICHAEL DARLING	Joseph Taylor
CAPTAIN HOOK and MR DARLING	Andrew C. Wadsworth
TINKER BELL and LOST WIFE GWENDOLYN	Joanna Woodward

Directed by Phil Willmott
Musical direction by Isaac McCullough
Choreography by Racky Plews
Musical supervision by Mark Collins
Designed by Phil Lindley

CHARACTERS

19+ roles (12 male, 8 female) can be divided between a cast of 12 or over with additional soldiers, nurses, music hall performers, street walkers, Lost Boys and their wives added for larger companies.

12 NAMED MALE ROLES

Captain George Llewellyn Davies/Peter Pan

Corporal Biggs
Sergeant Mullins

John Darling
Michael Darling

Lost Boy Tootles
Lost Boy Nibs
Lost Boy Slightly
Lost Boy Curly
Lost Boy Twin 1
Lost Boy Twin 2

J. M. Barrie/Captain Hook/Mr Darling

PLUS Additional Soldiers, Lost Boys and Music Hall Performers as required

8 NAMED FEMALE ROLES

Wendy Darling
Tinker Bell
Tiger Lilly

Lost Wife Gwendolyn
Lost Wife Cissie
Lost Wife Lady Edith
Lost Wife Mabel

Additional Lost Wives, Music Hall Performers, Street Girls, Can Can Dancers and Nurses as required

ORIGINAL DOUBLING FOR A CAST OF TWELVE (INC COSTUME PLOT)

Most characters speak eloquently in RP
Corporal Biggs, **Sergeant Mullins** and **Tinker Bell** have a London accent.

1. **Captain George Llewellyn Davies** in reality and **Peter Pan** in the dream
   (M, early twenties. Officer Class, efficient and emotionally reserved. Peter develops from a impetuous savage to a troubled young man before ending up as a caring, principled, and successful adult)
   Costume: Officer's Uniform, Edwardian Evening Wear

2. **Soldier** and **Lost Boy Nibs**
   (M, early twenties. Nibs is excitable but dim)
   Costume: Soldier's Uniform, Edwardian Evening Wear

3. **Soldier** and **Lost Boy Slightly**
   (M, early twenties. Slightly is cautious but eager to please)
   Costume: Soldier's Uniform, Edwardian Evening Wear

4. **Wendy Darling**
   (F, early twenties. Romantic yet resourceful)
   Costume: Edwardian Evening Wear, Day Dress, Red Cross Nurse's Uniform

5. **Soldier, Lost Boy Twin 1** and **Michael Darling** in the dream.
   (M, early twenties. Michael is endearing and passionate)
   Costume: Soldier's Uniform, Dressing Gown over Acrobat's Costume, Edwardian Evening Wear

6. **Soldier, Lost Boy Curly** and **John Darling** in the dream
   (M, early twenties. John is intense and quirky)
   Costume: Soldier's Uniform, Edwardian Evening Wear, Day Wear

7. **Soldier, Tootles**
   (M, early twenties. A dim, alpha male, aristocrat)
   Costume: Soldier's Uniform, Edwardian Evening Wear, Officer's Uniform

8. **Lost Wife Gwendolyn** and **Tinker Bell** and **A Music Hall Girl** and **Cancan Dancer 1**
(F, early twenties. Tinker Bell is feisty, obsessive, damaged)
Costume: Edwardian Evening Wear, Music Hall Girl, Shabby Whore, Cancan Costume

9. **Lost Wife Cissie** and a **Music Hall & Street Girl** and **Tiger Lilly** and **Pirate Show Girl.**
(F, early twenties. Tiger Lilly is Exotic and formidable)
Costume: Edwardian Evening Wear, Music Hall Girl, Tiger Lilly's S&M-Inspired Nightclub Act Costume, Edwardian Lady's Day Wear, Red Cross Nurse's Uniform, Pirate Showgirl

10. **Lost Wife Lady Edith** and a **Music Hall & Street Girl** and **Cancan Dancer 2**
(F, early twenties. Imposing but caring)
Costume: Edwardian Evening Wear, Music Hall Girl, Edwardian Lady's Day Wear, Can-can Costume, Red Cross Nurse's Uniform, Pirate Showgirl

11. **Lost Wife Mabel** and **Lost Boy Twin 2** and a **Music Hall & Street Girl** and **Cancan Dancer 3**
(F, early twenties. Twin 1 is male and eager to please. Mabel is practical but jolly)
Costume: Edwardian Gent's Evening Wear, Edwardian Lady's Evening Wear, Music Hall Girl, Edwardian Lady's Day Wear, Cancan Costume, Red Cross Nurse's Uniform, Pirate Showgirl

12. **J. M. Barrie** and **Captain Hook** and **Mr Darling**
(M, any age from thirty-five plus. Dilapidated yet charismatic and menacing)
Costume: Edwardian Evening Wear, Music Hall Magician's Costume, Wretched Opium Den Costume, Splendid But Homemade-in-the-Barracks Traditional Captain Hook Outfit.

Other parts to be allocated from within the Company:
Corporal Biggs in reality
Sergeant Mullins in reality

SETTING

The show has been conceived to work equally effectively with –
An empty stage and shifting shafts of light...
Or a complex, expensive set...
Or anything in between.

However, its designed scenes should flow from one to the other without "scene change" breaks.

SCENE AND SONG BREAKDOWN

*Indicates choreography

ACT ONE

PROLOGUE

J.M. Barrie's Introduction
Characters: J.M. Barrie, Soldiers

SCENE ONE

Soldiers staggering through the battlefield. George comforts an anxious Corporal Biggs. George/Peter then meets an adult Wendy.
Characters: Entire Company, Sergeant Mullins, Corporal Biggs, Wendy, George/Peter
Songs: **LOST** (Soldiers), **BLUE LAGOON** (George/Peter and Wendy)

SCENE TWO

Lord Tooterdge's house: Lost Boys Reunion. Wendy disapproves of their boyish behaviour and heads to the LWC. The boys talk about marriage.
Characters: George/Peter, Tootles, The Twins, Slightly, Nibs, Curly, Wendy
Songs: **LOST BOYS REUNION*** (The Lost Boys)

SCENE THREE

The Lost Wives discuss the hardships of marrying a Lost Boy. Tootles reveals that Peter is seeking Mr Darling's permission to marry Wendy.
Characters: Wendy, Edith, Cissie, Mabel, Gwendolyn, Tootles
Songs: **LOVING A LOST BOY** (The Lost Wives)

SCENE FOUR

A heated confrontation between George/Peter and Mr Darling. John tries to sway his father, but to no avail. Peter proposes to Wendy.

Characters: Wendy, George/Peter, Mr Darling, John
*Songs: **MARRY ME*** (George/Peter) and ***LOVING A LOST CHILD***
(Mr Darling)

SCENE FIVE

John and George/Peter talk in the hall. They discuss George/Peter's dreams.
Characters: John, George/Peter

SCENE SIX

Backstage at the music hall, John takes George/Peter to meet
Michael. Wendy enters after Michael's song and agrees to marry
Peter in the morning.
Characters: John, Michael, George/Peter, Showgirls, Lost Boys,
Wendy, Voice Call Boy
*Songs: **MUSIC HALL*** (Michael, The Company except Wendy
and Hook)*

SCENE SEVEN

Music hall auditorium. Entire Company gathers to watch
Michael's trapeze act. A magician puts on a captivating show,
but it would seem that only Wendy is privy to his true identity
Characters: Entire Company, Wendy, George/Peter, Chairman,
Hook, John, Nibs, Curly
*Songs: **SMOKE AND MIRRORS*** (Hook), ***A SLEIGHT OF HAND***
(Hook and Music Hall Girls)

SCENE EIGHT

Foyer after the show. Tootles shows up and tries to persuade
George/Peter to enlist. Tootles tells Wendy that the Lost Boys
are going to take their chief out for one final night of debauchery
before he ties the knot. Wendy has a bad feeling about it all.
Characters: John, Michael George/Peter, Wendy, Tootles

SCENE NINE

Lost Boys sing ***WE ARE THE LOST BOYS***

Characters: Lost Boys, Tootles, Curly, Nibs
*Songs: **WE ARE THE LOST BOYS**** (Lost Boys)

SCENE TEN

The Darling's house. John finds his father carrying a bundle of love letters.
Characters: John, Mr Darling

SCENE ELEVEN

Lost Boys tired and drunk on the street. Lost Boys leave George/Peter and Tootles to go home. Tootles insists on George/Peter having a 'dress rehearsal' before he marries Wendy. George/Peter meets Tinker Bell who takes him back to her room above an opium den.
Characters: George/Peter, Tootles, Lost Boys, Whores, Tinker Bell.
*Songs: **SLIP INTO THE DARKNESS**** (Tinker Bell, Whores and Men)

SCENE TWELVE

The wedding. Mr Darling shows up and gives Wendy his blessing. Tinker Bell bursts in and reveals that she and Peter had spent the night together. Wendy is distraught and tells Peter she never wants to see him again. The scene fades back to the trenches where Biggs and Mullins are trying to wake George. They leave him be.
Characters: Everyone, Wendy, Edith, Tootles, Mr Darling, John, Tinker Bell, Mullins, Biggs
*Songs: **THE WEDDING** (All), **WENDY'S EXIT** (Wendy)

SCENE THIRTEEN

Street outside the Darlings' residence. Mr Darling and John find George/Peter lying on the doorstep. Mr Darling chastises him, whilst John expresses his pacifistic objections to the war. George/Peter promises to prove himself a man and worthy of Wendy's affections by joining the army.
Characters: George/Peter, John, Mr Darling

SCENE FOURTEEN

George/Peter steels himself to war.
Character: Whole Company
*Songs: **ONCE MORE** (All)*

ACT TWO

SCENE ONE

The Darlings' house. John sings a song about interpreting dreams. George/Peter is yet to find his shadow.
Characters: Entire Company except Hook, George/Peter, John
*Songs: **JUNGIAN DREAM ANALYSIS*** (All except Hook)

SCENE TWO

The opium den. Tinker Bell finds Hook and it becomes clear that they had a pre-arranged bargain – she gives him Peter Pan and she gets her wings back. Hook forges a plan to have Pan's own comrades turn against him. Tinker Bell soon realises she was never going to get her wings back from Hook.
Characters: Hook, George/Peter (voice), Tinker Bell
*Songs: **DRAGONS** (Hook)*

SCENE THREE

The streets of Paris. The Lost Boys have one last night of revelling before they go to war at dawn.
Characters: Lost Boys, Michael
*Songs: **BOYS IN PARIS** (Lost Boys), **MICHAEL IN PARIS** (Michael)*

SCENE FOUR

Shadowland Nightclub. Tiger Lilly, an exotic cabaret dancer, takes to the stage and performs her song. George/Peter leaves for fresh air.
Characters: Lost Boys, Tiger Lilly, Mc, Tootles, George/Peter
*Songs: **OOH LA LA** (Tiger Lilly leads the Company)*

SCENE FIVE

George/Peter meets Tiger Lilly in an alley way outside the club. Peter confides in Tiger Lilly that he wants to prove to Wendy he can be a man. Tiger Lilly is certain that she can reason with Wendy.
Characters: George/Peter

SCENE SIX

John is trying to recruit passers-by to his peace corps. The crowd turns on John, but Tinker Bell shows up just in time to help him escape.
Characters: John, Tinker Bell, Passers-by
Songs: **UNITE** (John)

SCENE SEVEN

Tinker Bell desperately tries to tell John of Hook's plan, but he is hearing none of it.
Characters: John, Tinker Bell

SCENE EIGHT

The Darlings' house. Wendy, having read Tiger Lilly's letter, believes Peter is truly remorseful and packs her bags with the intention of returning to him. John agrees to accompany her and they form a Kensington Gardens division of the Red Cross. Wendy comes up with the idea of training dogs to act as messengers.
Characters: Wendy, John, Tinker Bell
Songs: *Wendy's Song* (Wendy)

SCENE NINE

The Lost Wives, John and Wendy sing Unite.
Characters: The Lost Wives, Edith, John, Wendy
Songs: **UNITE** (Reprise)

SCENE TEN

The battlefield. Everyone leaves the stage except Michael who breaks down in shellshock.
Characters: Entire Company, Michael
Songs: **LOST** (Reprise), **MUSIC HALL** (Reprise)

SCENE ELEVEN

Red Cross military hospital. The Lost Wives sing as they tend to the wounded and ask if the war was worth it. Wendy presses Tootles to let her see Peter, but he insists the captain is still too busy. Edith brings a sick Tinker Bell into the ward. Tinker Bell begs Wendy to let her see Peter. Wendy concedes after listening to the fairy's story but too late to stop the ex-fairy fading away.
Characters: Edith, Cissie, Mabel, Nurses, Wendy, Michael, Wounded Soldiers, Tootles, Tinker Bell
Songs: **FIRST AID** (The Lost Wives), **BELL'S STORY** (Tinker Bell)

SCENE TWELVE

The officers' quarters. Tootles informs George/Peter he needs a costume for the officers' mess fancy dress party. George/Peter discovers that Wendy has been trying to visit him. Hook enters and reveals that he has been behind the war the entire time in a vaudeville routine. Peter is racked with guilt. Wendy, John and Michael enter, closely followed by Edith, and George/Peter shoots Hook.
Characters: Tootles, George/Peter, Hook, John, Michael, Wendy
Songs: **GEORGE/PETER'S SONG** (tune **SHADOWS**), **WHAT ABOUT ME AND YOU?*** (Hook with Show Girls and the Wounded), **BEING A MAN** (Wendy)

SCENE THIRTEEN

The trenches. George tells Sergeant Mullins to get the troops prepared for battle. Everyone sings to him and he changes his mind and calls a retreat.
Characters: Entire Company, George, Mullins, Wendy, Tinker Bell, Michael, John, J.M. Barrie
Songs: **BLUE LAGOON** (Reprise)

THE PRESS ON LOST BOY

★ ★ ★ ★

"This is a brilliant musical. A spectacular triumph"
Everything Theatre

In *Lost Boy*, writer Phil Willmott sets out to address
the death of innocence of young men during the First
World War. He has hit upon an original way to do this:
by imagining Peter Pan as a captain in the British army,
travelling to the front line to fight for the glory of his
country, but mainly for the heart of his childhood love,
Wendy Darling.
WhatsOnStage

"Epic themes and riveting drama. Artfully structured
and packed with strong musical numbers that drive the
narrative"
The Stage

"The piece is near on flawless in its execution – a big, bright
and energetic affair"
Exeunt

"Phil Willmott's *Lost Boy* offers an imaginative sequel to
Peter Pan. This is a bold attempt to marry the worlds of
childhood fantasy and adult nightmare. This is a far more
enjoyable new British musical than *Stephen Ward*, playing
down the road. Willmott's songs are tuneful and witty"
Sunday Express

"Willmott's staging excels"
Musical Theatre Review

"It is early days yet – there is still time for it to relax into a
knockout West End musical"
Remotegoat

"Thought-provoking and inspiring – an excellent production
with an outstanding cast in a bold new sequel to
J.M. Barrie's *Peter Pan*"
Theatre Net

"Mapping the death of innocence. Willmott's vigorous reimagining of the fates of Pan and friends"
Extra Extra

"Timely and thought-provoking – an accomplished work of considerable imagination"
Theatre World Magazine

"Willmott's big theme is the death of innocence, a subject for which he finds a powerful dramatic metaphor as he imagines the Boy who wouldn't grow up signing up for 'An Awfully Big Adventure' and finally discovering what it means to be 'A Man' on the battlefields of France"
Metro

"Packed with big ideas. In part an elegy for lost innocence but it's a lot more than that. The mostly youthful cast is admirably vigorous. Grace Gardner has a showstopping number as Wendy, and no one makes a keener impression than Joseph Taylor, as her brother Michael"
Evening Standard

"A bold and original idea.
The show is blessed with a score that elicits tears and laughter in equal measure"
West End Frame

"Thought-provoking and frequently disturbing – a powerful start to a year of great drama planned nationally to commemorate the centenary of the start of the Great War"
The Bucks Herald

"Entertaining, thought-provoking and beautifully performed...and some fine songs"
BroadwayWorld

"A musical that will leave a lasting impression. Phil Willmott's anthem to the corruption of innocence and lost youth makes compelling viewing"
Leighton Buzzard Observer

"Fantastic and fantastical.
Phil Willmott's poignant musical is full of good ideas...
The darkness of the show's vision is compelling and the cast
attack the material with gusto"
Guardian

"A bold reimagining of the Peter Pan story.
Willmott's proposal that Edwardian society ill prepared
young men for the complexities of maturity is interesting
and his interweaving of dream, fiction and reality
innovative... the music, drawing on styles of the period, is
beautifully delivered by three onstage musicians (keyboard,
cello and clarinet), and while some songs are witty ('Jungian
Dream Analysis'), others are suddenly touching (a trio
by three Nurses on coping with the horrors of the front).
Willmott's staging is polished and the fine 12-strong cast,
led by Steven Butler's agonised George, fill the space with
song"
Financial Times

"Excellent songs. Very good performances"
Life In The Cheap Seats

"A thought-provoking and bittersweet musical that tracks
the demise of innocence in war epic themes and belting
musical numbers. *Lost Boy* is a truly great way to start the
first year of the First World War centenary"
What's On London

"An intriguing set-up... Resonates powerfully"
Time Out

"An ambitious and complex work. This is a stimulating
start to a year which will see the First World War often
memorialised and sets a standard for other shows to match"
British Theatre Guide

ACT ONE

Prologue

J. M. BARRIE People always ask me, "Mr Barrie, where did the idea to write *Peter Pan* come from?" I change the subject if I can, but the truth is I had adopted five real-life Lost Boys of my own and the make-believe of their childhood inspired the fearless, fearsome figure of Pan. A boy who never...wouldn't, couldn't grow up. Was it wrong to wish the same for my sons?

Of the three, George held onto Peter Pan the longest. I noticed him inventing little games and stories about his hero long after his brothers had left such things behind.

Soldiers enter into the darkness.

So when the great terrible war seduced a whole nation of Lost Boys with promise of adventure, I gave him a little copy of *Peter Pan* for the journey.

By 1916, rumours began to trickle home that the awfully big adventure to which we'd consigned our young men was not the blaze of glory we'd imagined.

All I could do was wait for news and prey my little Neverland flight of fancy gave him some comfort.

Scene One

A bedraggled regiment of exhausted young soldiers are staggering through a First World War battlefield. They are led by **CAPTAIN GEORGE LLEWELYN DAVIES** *and include* **CORPORAL BIGGS** *and* **SERGEANT MULLINS.**

SONG: "LOST"

GEORGE	CHORUS
DEAR LORD, MAKE IT STOP!	
CONSTANT GREY, ENDLESS MUD.	HMM
NO MAN'S LAND, BLEAK,	HMM
EERIE, SILENT AND PAID FOR IN BLOOD.	HMM

GEORGE AND CHORUS

EVERY BREATH SEEMS TO KNOW,
THAT IT COULD BE MY LAST.
IF I STUMBLE AND FALL NOW,
DEATH WILL CATCH UP WITH ME FAST.

GEORGE	CHORUS
THE GREY'S CLOSING IN	HMM
I AM FINISHED,	HMM
EXTINGUISHED,	HMM
IF I DIE, AT LEAST IT MEANS I'LL SLEEP—	HMM

GEORGE Alright lads, we'll rest here for a few hours. We push on at day break.

SERGEANT MULLINS Captain Davis?

GEORGE Yes, Sergeant.

SERGEANT MULLINS There's a problem with Corporal Biggs, Sir. He's not doing so well. He's refusing to obey orders.

GEORGE *(irritated)* Hell's teeth! Bring him over.

He does.

SERGEANT MULLINS *(to* **BIGGS***)* Report to Captain Davis now.

CORPORAL BIGGS Yes, Sarge.

    BIGGS *approaches* **GEORGE.**

GEORGE What's the matter, Corporal?

CORPORAL BIGGS They're saying it's suicide, Sir, the others, to press on like this under fire. I can't, I promised the wife I'd come home safe and sound. We've a baby on the way. What's she going to say if... I don't want to die, Sir!

GEORGE Now listen here. These are our orders, Corporal.

CORPORAL BIGGS But I don't want to be blown to pieces, Sir.

GEORGE Then your best bet is to follow those orders, Sam. The generals know what they're doing. Do you think they're just going to throw you into enemy fire if they don't think there's a good chance we can capture that ridge?

CORPORAL BIGGS But what if they're wrong, Sir?

GEORGE Now, listen here. We don't think like that in the British army. We follow orders. It's the way things work. How would it be if it was every man for himself? We follow orders. That way everyone stands a chance of getting home alive.

CORPORAL BIGGS *(reassured)* Yes, Sir.

GEORGE And I promise you, I promise you, I will get us out of this alive. Now you make sure you tell the others.

CORPORAL BIGGS Yes, Sir.

GEORGE Good man, I know I can rely on you. *(gets an idea)* In fact you take the first watch, wake me in an hour and I'll take over. Do you think you can manage that?

CORPORAL BIGGS Yes, Sir.

GEORGE That's the best cure for a few jitters. Responsibility. And obeying orders. You're shaking, Corporal.

CORPORAL BIGGS Yes, Sir, sorry, Sir.

GEORGE *(kindly)* Think about something else, think about home, being safe, back before all this.

CORPORAL BIGGS Is that what you do, Sir?

GEORGE Sometimes.

CORPORAL BIGGS Is it true your father wrote *Peter Pan*, Sir?

GEORGE Not this again... Why does everyone... My adoptive father, yes.

CORPORAL BIGGS That's wonderful. I'm going to be sure and tell the wife. You got a wife, Sir?

GEORGE *(sharp)* Don't be impertinent, Corporal.

CORPORAL BIGGS Sorry, Sir.

GEORGE *(sharp)* And stop shaking! *(relenting. Kindly)* No, I'm not married. *(to amuse him)* I used to dream I'd grow up to be Peter Pan so that I could marry Wendy.

CORPORAL BIGGS Wendy? From the book?

GEORGE Yes.

CORPORAL BIGGS That's nice, Sir.

GEORGE Calmer now?

CORPORAL BIGGS Yes, Sir.

GEORGE Good man, now keep a sharp look out, I'm relying on you.

CORPORAL BIGGS Yes, Sir. You can rely on me.

GEORGE Good man.

SONG: "BLUE LAGOON"

CORPORAL BIGGS *(leaving)* Sleep well, Sir. Dream of Never Land.

GEORGE That's it, dream the grey away. *(to make the corporal smile)* Maybe Wendy will marry me tonight.

Now he is alone, a vision of **WENDY** *appears. She is in her early twenties.*

WENDY *(sings)*
> JUST SEE THE BLUE,
> A BLUE YOU KNEW LONG AGO.
> A BLUE LAGOON
> BENEATH THOSE CLOUDLESS SKIES,
> WHEN IT FELT GRAND
> TO STAND, THAT SUN IN YOUR EYES,
> THEN RACE EACH OTHER OUT
> ACROSS THE SAND,
> YOU'D FLY.

GEORGE *(spoken)* Wendy?!

WENDY *(sings)*
> CLIMB HIGH TO DIVE
> INTO THE TURQUOISE BELOW,
> THE WATER WARM,
> THE MERMAIDS' SONG SUBLIME,
> REACH FOR THE BLUE,
> THOSE CHILDHOOD SUMMERS ARE GONE
> BUT BATHE IN BRILLIANT BLUE
> ONE FINAL TIME.

GEORGE
> THEY PROMISED US ADVENTURE,
> IT'S NIGHTMARE, NOT ADVENTURE.
> THERE'S ONLY MUD,
> THERE'S ONLY KHAKI AND GREY
> SLICED THROUGH WITH WIRE,
> THE ONLY HOPE'S TO PRAY.
> BUT PRAYERS ARE LOST
> AMONGST THE ROAR OF THE GUN
> I WANT TO RUN, TO WEEP,
> NOT DIE THIS WAY.

WENDY

LOOK AGAIN,
THE HORROR YOU SEE WILL DIMINISH.

GEORGE

NOT THE GREY.

WENDY

YES, THINGS ARE BLEAK
BUT YOU CAN DECIDE HOW THINGS FINISH.

GEORGE

WE CAN ONLY PRAY.

WENDY

THIS IS THE MOMENT
WHEN YOU CAN DECIDE HOW IT ENDS.

GEORGE

WHEN WILL IT END?

WENDY

LOST IN THE DARK, WITHOUT STRENGTH, WITHOUT HOPE,
    WITHOUT FRIENDS –
OR DREAM ONCE MORE,
DREAM THAT YOU'RE PETER AGAIN
AND TRY TO LOOK
THE WAY YOU USED TO SEE.
DON'T CHOOSE THE GREY, THE DARK,
THE RATS AND THE RAIN,
JUST BELIEVE
THE BLUE CAN SET YOU FREE.

WENDY *places her hand onto* **PETER**'s *knee.*

(spoken) Wake up now. Wake up as Peter Pan. Is it working?

Beat. Then – the sound of a bird singing.

GEORGE

A BLUE BIRD SINGS.

WENDY

YES, YES, YOU'RE GETTING IT NOW.

GEORGE

    IT SOUNDS LIKE HOPE.

WENDY

    REMEMBER IF YOU CAN

GEORGE

    LOOK! OVER THERE,
    BLUEBELLS BREAK OUT ALL AROUND,

WENDY *and* **GEORGE**

    ALL NATURE BOWS TO YOU.

GEORGE

    I'M PETER PAN,
    I'M PETER PAN,
    AT LAST I'M PETER PAN!

PETER Wendy, ha! Look at you. Your eyes are the same but you're—

WENDY A woman. Do you like it?

PETER I don't know. It's strange. Yes, I think I do.

WENDY I've grown up.

PETER How could you? It's against orders, punishable by death!

WENDY But you weren't around. You wouldn't fly back with us to London.

PETER Good job if it makes you all lumpy. How do you expect to steal up on pirates?

WENDY I've never been called upon to do so and changing is a part of growing up. For instance, I am pleased to see you've grown a little stout. It suits you. Very distinguished like the king and quite suitable now pirates are no longer our concern.

PETER Do the pirates run wild in London then?

WENDY I don't think so. I expect they have to work in offices nowadays.

PETER What is offices?

WENDY It's a place where you go to make money.

PETER Like when we made porridge? Out of kisses.

WENDY I don't... No, that was acorns. Don't you see... Yes, yes we made porridge out of the acorns we thought were kisses. But...grown-ups have a different sort of kiss.

PETER What for? Do you happen to have one on your person?

WENDY My first one. I haven't used it up yet. I've been saving it for you. Close your eyes.

He does.

PETER What are you doing?

WENDY That is what grown-ups call a kiss.

PETER They don't give one another acorns?

WENDY Rarely. Or thimbles.

She kisses him.

PETER I think I may like it. Do you have another I might try?

They kiss again.

I like these new type of kisses better. Do you know where we can get a supply?

WENDY I have more then you'll ever need. You shall have one when you wake every morning, and when you return to me every evening from the office.

PETER Where the pirates go?

WENDY Well, not just pirates.

PETER Will there be adventure?

WENDY It is not a place one goes to for adventure.

PETER Then what is the point of it?

WENDY You go there so your children might eat.

PETER Our children! How are they? John and Michael, and Nibs and Slightly and Tootles, Curly and the twins. I should like us to play Mother and Father again and watch you make them take their medicine.

WENDY It was only make-believe. They should not like to be called our children now.

PETER *(feet apart, hands on hips)* Then I shall teach them some manners.

WENDY Peter, no, things have changed. There's a lot you don't understand about the grown-up world. For instance, please stop standing like that. Grown men don't unless they're in an operetta.

SONG: "NORMAL"

PETER I am Peter Pan, I know everything. And what I don't know is silly.

WENDY No, no, growing up is the greatest of adventures. I'll show you how to do it. Like you showed me how to reach Never Land. You've a man's body now. It must be because you've left Never Land behind. Peter, are you listening?

PETER The new type of kiss. It has bewitched me. It's all I can think about. Must I take horrid medicine with a spoon?

WENDY It's normal. Adults are very fond of kisses.

PETER I think I like this...this "normal".

WENDY I wonder. Could you ever live a real life?

PETER Show me how.

WENDY You want to be normal?

PETER I do, I do.

WENDY You don't really know what it means, do you?

PETER No. But growing up will be my next adventure!

WENDY What kind of man do you think you'll be?

PETER One that lives on fresh air and kisses.

SONG: "NORMAL"

WENDY

NORMAL ISN'T EASY
ALL WE'VE BEEN THROUGH
MEANS IT WILL BE A STRUGGLE TO ADAPT
CAN YOU LEAVE A CHILDHOOD SPENT IN SOMEWHERE SO
    MAGNIFICENT
THAT YOU COULD SAVE A FAIRY IF YOU CLAPPED?
ALAS WE CAN'T ESCAPE THE WORLD'S ATTENTION
THERE'S BEEN A BOOK ABOUT US AND I KNOW
EV'RY PARENT IN THE LAND'S PUT IT IN THEIR CHILDREN'S
    HAND
BUT YOU AND I MUST LET THE STORY GO.

KEEP NEVERLAND WITHIN YOUR HEART
BUT SAFE BEYOND A STAR
DON'T FORGET ITS LEGACY
HAS MADE US WHO WE ARE.
THOUGH GROWING UP MEANS TURNING FROM THE CHILDISH
    THINGS WE KNOW
WE'LL STILL REMEMBER
OUR DECEMBER
OF MAGIC LONG AGO.

PETER

IS EVERYONE FROM NEVERLAND NOW NORMAL?

WENDY

SOME STILL FIND IT TRICKY TO ADAPT
JOHN AND MICHAEL STRUGGLE MOST,
BUT CURLY, NIBBS, AND SLIGHTLY BOAST
OF DOING WELL THOUGH OFTEN FEELING TRAPPED.
TOOTLES MARRIED WELL TO LADY EDITH
HE'S AS CONSERVATIVE AS YOU CAN GET

MOST ARE SETTLED WITH A WIFE
AND TRY TO LIVE A NORMAL LIFE
BUT NONE OF THEM FORGET

COMPANY

NEVERLAND IS PART OF US,
STILL JUST BEYOND A STAR
THOUGH WE'VE GROWN TO ADULTHOOD,
IT MADE US WHO WE ARE
DEEP WITHIN OUR HEART'S A SECRET NO ONE NEEDS TO
    KNOW

WENDY Welcome to adulthood, Peter.

COMPANY

WE STILL REMEMBER
THAT DECEMBER
OF MAGIC LONG AGO

PETER The other orphans from Never Land? The Lost
Boys...have they grown up already?

WENDY Oh yes. It's at the end of our book. You can see the twins,
Nibs and Curly any day going to an office, each carrying a
little bag and an umbrella. Tootles married a lady of title,
and so he became a lord. Slightly went into the law –

PETER So all the little savages we lived with underground
are "normal" now?

WENDY Well...most of the time!

End of scene

Scene Two

LORD TOOTERIDGE (**TOOTLES'**) *house.*

The **LOST BOYS**, *now in their early twenties, burst boisterously on to the stage in evening dress.*

At the centre is **TOOTLES** *himself. A bluff and strident rugger type. With him are* **SLIGHTLY, CURLY, NIBBS,** *and the* **TWINS.**

SONG: "LOST BOYS REUNION"

LOST BOYS

> IT'S A LOST BOYS REUNION
> HERE IN KENSINGTON GARDENS,
> THROUGH THE WORKING WEEK
> WE'RE RESPECTABLE AS HELL.
> BUT WE LIKE TO GET TOGETHER
> AND REMEMBER THE OLD DAYS
> WHEN ADVENTURES
> NOT ACCOUNT BOOKS
> WERE OUR GODS!
> WE WERE LITTLE SODS.
>
> EDWARDIAN GENTLEMEN DON'T
> GET TO SLAUGHTER PIRATES.
> WE'VE NEVER SEEN A CROCODILE
> TRAVERSING THE THAMES.
> IT'S HARD SOMETIMES TO TOW THE LINE,
> FORGETTING ANY VIOLENCE.

SLIGHTLY

> SO WE GET DRUNK
> AND TOOLED UP
> FRIDAY NIGHT.

ALL

> AND IT'S TIME TO FIGHT!

They see GEORGE *(who they regard as the adult* PETER
PAN*) and* WENDY. *They are delighted.*

PETER Hello, boys!

TOOTLES My word! Do my eyes deceive me?!

THE TWINS We don't believe it!

PETER Hello, twins! Hello, Slightly!

SLIGHTLY You came back.

NIBS Are you going to grow up now, like us?

PETER Yes, Nibs. What's it like?

TOOTLES Awful. That's why we meet every Friday night and
go a bit wild in your honour.

LAST WEEKEND IN KILBURN
WE WERE RUCKING WITH THE IRISH,

NIBS
FROM TIME TO TIME ON LONDON BRIDGE,
WE LAY INTO SOME ROUGHS.

TOOTLES
THERE'S NO EXHILARATION
IN A WEEK SPENT IN THE CITY,

TWINS
SO FRIDAY NIGHT,
WE'RE ON THE STREETS,
ENJOYING FISTICUFFS.

PETER
TIME TO HAVE A NEW KIND OF ADVENTURE
NOT SUITED TO A BOY BUT FOR A MAN.
WENDY HAS BEEN SPEAKING
OF A SHIP KNOWN AS THE OFFICE,
WHERE PIRATES DO NOT FEAR THE NAME OF PAN.
JOIN ME AS WE STORM THE WRETCHED VESSEL,
DRIVE THE VILLAINS BACK THEN HEADS'LL ROLL,

MAKE EM UNDERSTAND
THAT JUST LIKE NEVER LAND
THE OFFICE IS IN PETER PAN'S CONTROL.

SLIGHTLY

WE COULD STAB A FOUNTAIN PEN,
INTO THE BOSSES HEART

TWINS

DROWN HIM IN A VAT OF INK
AND PULL THE PLACE APART

NIBS

THEN AGAIN WE'D GET THE SACK
WHICH WOULDN'T DO, OH WELL

ALL

BETTER STICK TO FRIDAY NIGHT
FOR RAISING MERRY HELL.
IT'S A LOST BOYS REUNION
HERE IN KENSINGTON GARDENS,
THROUGH THE WORKING WEEK
WE'RE RESPECTABLE AS HELL
BUT FRIDAY NIGHT WE LIKE TO MEET
RECAPTURING THE OLD DAYS
WHEN ADVENTURES
NOT ACCOUNT BOOKS
WERE OUR GODS!
WE WERE LITTLE SODS.

Slowing.

GROWING OLDER'S TOUGH,
ALL THAT RESPONSIBILITY.

Picking up.

WITH THE BOYS, OUT PICKING FIGHTS
IS WHERE I WANT TO BE!

TOOTLES *(to* **PETER***)* We knew you'd come back, old man. The moment war was declared. We all said – this'll bring him back to us. The gang together again – going into battle side by side behind our illustrious leader. What are your orders, Sir? When do we sign up?

WENDY Not so fast, Tootles. He's not a bloodthirsty delinquent any more, even if you lot still are.

TOOTLES Of course he is. You'll never change, will you, old boy?

PETER We shall decorate the office walls with pirate scalps.

SLIGHTLY I'm not sure Miss Prendergast would approve.

TWINS They get cross if you move the filing.

PETER From there we will plot new expeditions and apply war paint.

NIBS They do stipulate a dark necktie at all times.

TOOTLES It's the end of the quarter but I'll check with my secretary for an opening.

PETER From where we will think happy thoughts and fly to tease mermaids.

SLIGHTLY I'm not sure the Lord Chancellor would like that.

CURLY I'm sure I read a regulation discouraging high spirits during office hours.

TOOTLES Best stick to Friday nights, old chap. You'll get the hang of things soon. But if we enlist. That'd be a different matter.

WENDY Tootles, he's only just got here.

CURLY But you will let him out to play with us, tonight? It's Friday night.

NIBS You could join us too, Wendy.

WENDY Out with you little beasts, comparing automobiles and flatulence? I think not.

SLIGHTLY We don't always talk about flatulence.

WENDY Of course not, Slightly. There has to be interruptions while you drink.

NIBS Doesn't stop him farting though.

Boys roar approval.

WENDY Why don't I leave you children to catch up while I say hello to Edith and the LWC.

PETER What is LWC?

ALL The Lost Wives Club.

TOOTLES The ladies like to gather for cosy chats whilst we men folk are out carousing.

WENDY I won't be long, Peter. Don't let them talk you into anything. *(not optimistic)* And, gentlemen, if you could help Peter understand a little of life in London.

TWINS Leave it to us, Wendy.

WENDY *(to* **PETER***)* Father has been so withdrawn since Mother died, but I'm sure he'll make you welcome.

NIBS Six months after Wendy invited us to stay, he had us packed off to an orphanage.

WENDY He was different then. His grief was...

PETER I shall make this old man see the cleverness of me! Has he wrestled a bear? Ridden wild horses with Indian braves? Can he cut a pirate throat in the blink of an eye so he bleeds to death in slow agony with the name of Pan on his lips?

Beat.

SLIGHTLY Well, good luck with that, Wendy.

NIBS Yes, good luck.

PETER *(affectionately to* **WENDY***)* Dear Old Lady.

TWINS We remember when he used to call her that.

PETER *(continuing)* Peter Pan, vanquisher of brigands and conqueror of office pirates, will make you proud. *(They* *kiss.)* Hey, boys, did you learn the new kissing? Better then acorns. You should try.

Lining up to kiss WENDY.

NIBS Well, I don't mind if I do.

TWINS Us next!

PETER *snarls at them. Suddenly disconcertingly animalistic.*

WENDY Gentlemen! Please remember you're married men.

SLIGHTLY How do you stop a beautiful woman desiring you?

THE BOYS Marry her!

They roar with laughter.

WENDY I'll be sure and pass that on to Louisa, Slightly.

BOYS *mock react (Oooh!) to slightly being in trouble now.*

WENDY *exits.*

TOOTLES Peter, are you going to marry Wendy for real?

PETER What's "marry"?

TOOTLES Sort of claim her as your own. Let's other fellows know to back off.

PETER I should like that.

NIBS There's a ceremony.

PETER Like the Indians?

NIBS Sort of but with more aunts.

PETER Aunts? I have not heard of this. Are they giant ants?

NIBS No. *(beat)* Well, actually now you come to mention it...

TOOTLES Peter. I'm wondering, old chap, have you ever "known" a woman?

PETER Only the treacherous kind. A mother who never searched for me when I fell from my pram.

TOOTLES Yes, yes. No, I didn't mean all that. Have you ever "been" with a woman?

PETER Of course. My nanny took me to the gardens that day.

TOOTLES There's a few things a man should know.

PETER Like the new style kisses?

TOOTLES Yes, but believe me there's a bit more to it. To the library, I think, gentlemen, and those rather inspirational prints I had imported from Paris.

TWINS Show him the one with the twins!

PETER Peter Pan says "death to book learning". (**PETER** *often refers to himself in the third person.*)

TOOTLES I wouldn't make your mind up about that just yet, old son.

They all exit.

End of scene

Scene Three

WENDY, LADY EDITH TOOTERIDGE *and* **LOST WIVES CISSIE, MABLE** *and* **GWENDOLYN** *enter in evening wear.*

WENDY Peter? I'd like to you to meet Lady Edith, Tootles' wife – oh, they've gone.

CISSIE I expect they're playing billiards. Plotting their Friday night adventures.

EDITH Oh, let them be, Cissie. It's nice to have some peace.

MABEL Of course we've heard a great deal about your childhood escapades from our husbands. Are you sure this romantic attachment to the ring leader is wise?

EDITH Their missing hero returns, Mabel. They'll be uncontrollable now.

CISSIE The pack is complete.

MABEL Is that pack as in cards or pack as in wolves?

EDITH Wendy, my dear. It has become our tradition that whenever an ex-Lost Boy forms an attachment, we gather to offer the poor unfortunate girl a few words of advice. Alas, today our numbers are depleted, some of our members have been made frail by the trials they have faced, but that only makes our words all the more prescient, particularly as you have chosen the most spirited Lost Boy of them all. I fear for your sanity, my dear.

WENDY I don't understand?

EDITH *(prompting)* Mabel?

MABEL Life with a Lost Boy is not for the faint-hearted, Wendy. It requires stamina.

EDITH Determination.

GWENDOLYN And the patience of a saint.

EDITH Indeed it does. *(to* **WENDY***)* You see my dear – *(She sings.)*

SONG: *"LOVING A LOST BOY"*

LOVING A LOST BOY'S
NOT AS EASY AS IT MAY SEEM.
LOVE HIM A BIT TOO MUCH
AND HE'LL VANISH AGAIN LIKE
A SUMMER NIGHT'S DREAM.
YET WHEN HE NEEDS YOUR LOVE
YOU CAN'T EVER TURN YOUR BACK,
THE WIFE OF A LOST BOY
NEEDS THE WISDOM AND STRENGTH
HER HUSBAND WILL ALWAYS LACK.

LOST WIVES

THERE'LL BE PASSION LIKE THE POWER OF THE SUN,
BUT JUST AS QUICKLY HE WILL TURN AND RUN.
SOME NIGHTS HE WILL LOVE YOU
AND YOU'LL THINK HE'LL STAY FOR SURE

EDITH

BUT WHEN THE DAWN COMES YOU CAN BET
YOU'LL BE ALONE ONCE MORE.

SO LOVING A LOST BOY
IS NOT FOR THE FAINT OF HEART
THERE'S LAUGHTER AND THERE'S JOY
BUT HEARTACHE AND PAIN TOO,
RIGHT FROM THE START.
STUDY OUR SAD PLIGHT
LEARN EV'RY THING YOU CAN
FOR LOVING A LOST BOY
TAKES DOUBLE THE EFFORT
OF LOVING A NORMAL MAN.

MABEL

HE NEVER STOPS TO KISS HIS SON GOOD NIGHT,

GWENDOLYN

DON'T EXPECT HIM HOME BEFORE IT'S LIGHT,

CISSIE

HE'S NEVER LEARNT MY BIRTHDAY,

EDITH

COMMITMENTS MAKE HIM RUN

ALL LOST WIVES

A LOST BOY DANCES TO A DIFF'RENT TUNE FROM EVERYONE.

EDITH *(spoken)* Do you love him enough to endure it?

THE LOST WIVES

HE'LL LOVE YOU LIKE THE CRASHING OF THE WAVES
AND MAKE YOU FEEL LIKE EVERYTHING HE CRAVES
BUT LEARN NOT TO SURRENDER
FOR THE MOMENT THAT YOU DO
THE TIDE WILL TURN, HE'LL DISAPPEAR
WITHOUT A THOUGHT FOR YOU

SO, LOVING A LOST BOY
MEANS LEAVING YOUR OLD DREAMS,
NOTHING BUT HIM COUNTS
YOU LIVE KISS TO KISS,
OR THAT'S HOW IT SEEMS.
SOON YOU'LL BE MISTRESS OF
THE TRICKS THAT YOU MUST EMPLOY,

MABEL

LIKE SOME HELEN OF TROY,

CISSIE

BUT YOU'RE ONLY A TOY,

ALL

WHEN YOU'RE
LOVING A LOST,
LOVING A LOST—

WENDY *(interrupting, spoken)* He's not like the rest of them, not any more.

The **LWC** *look at each other knowingly and resolve the song.*

THE LOST WIVES

LOVING A LOST BOY.

TOOTLES *enters.*

TOOTLES Edith, have you seen those Cuban cigars? That new footman says there's none left.

EDITH You finished them at Christmas, dearest. How is Peter getting along?

TOOTLES Splendidly. In fact, we so excited him about the perks of marriage that he rushed off to get your father's permission, Wendy.

WENDY What?!

They freeze as the following scene is set up behind them.

End of scene

Scene Four

The **DARLINGS'** *house.*

A fuming **MR DARLING** *address* **PETER**. *They are both in evening wear.*

MR DARLING So correct me if I'm wrong. You've no family, no address, no prospects and you expect me to hand over my daughter.

PETER Yes, I am extremely keen to try sexual intercourse.

MR DARLING As you've made very clear.

They freeze as the previous scene is finished.

*

TOOTLES Romantic, ain't it.

EDITH Tootles, I sometimes doubt you've the brains you were born with. You know Mr Darling is still grieving for his wife.

TOOTLES The chief should be a breath of fresh air then.

They exit.

*

Back to the **DARLINGS'** *house.*

MR DARLING So correct me if I'm wrong. You've no family, no address, no prospects and you expect me to hand over my daughter.

PETER Yes, I am extremely keen to try sexual intercourse.

MR DARLING As you've made very clear.

PETER Don't worry, Tootles has shown me lithographs of the key positions and I know how it's done on the Paris Island. Peter Pan scoffed at this grappling at first but apparently it is most pleasant and the ladies welcome it as a sign of appreciation.

WENDY *rushes in. The sound of dogs barking.*

WENDY Ah, I see you two have already met. Peter, I wish you'd waited for me.

MR DARLING *(calling off)* Nana! For heaven's sake, will you keep those puppies quiet!

The sound of dogs stop.

PETER Wendy, this old pirate grows tiresome? Shall I kill him?

WENDY No, Peter! Please do not kill Father.

PETER Father? Peter Pan has never had a father.

MR DARLING You should know, young man, that I do share my late wife's delight in the perversities of Never land.

PETER Send him away and let's play at honeymoon. Tootles told me about it.

MR DARLING That is enough!

PETER Are you not pleased, Wendy? It is what grown-ups do.

MR DARLING How dare you defy me?

PETER How dare I? You grizzled pile of cod fish poo! It is for Peter Pan to ask the questions! It is for others to obey! Fetch me more scotch firewater! And rich, damp cake!

WENDY *(smiling in spite of herself)* Peter, you know that is the worst kind.

MR DARLING *(calling off)* John! John! A word with you now!

Dogs bark.

(He exits, yelling to the dogs.) Nana!

WENDY *looks sternly at* PETER.

PETER Wendy, I have displeased you. But...I do not know why. This new world, it's so strange to me and I see I am but a savage beast unfit for the company of "normal". But Peter Pan knows what he knows and—

PETER *sings to* **WENDY**—

SONG: "MARRY ME"

YOU MUST ALWAYS FACE YOUR ENEMIES
AND DIVE INTO THE DEEP
SOAR INTO SPACE AND RACE A SHOOTING STAR
WHEN IT'S RIGHT YOU FLY TILL MORNING
WHEN IT'S RIGHT YOU BEAR THE PAIN
WHEN SOMETHING'S RIGHT YOU SEE IT FROM AFAR
AND, WENDY, CAN'T YOU FEEL IT?
WE JUST ARE.

MARRY ME
LET'S START OUR LIFE TOGETHER
MARRY ME,
FOREVER AND A DAY.
I'M IN A SPIN ABOUT YOU
I SEE NOW THAT WITHOUT YOU
I'M A BOY
MAKE ME A MAN
AND MARRY ME.

BUT WHY SHOULD YOU?
I'LL ONLY LET YOU DOWN.
A CLUMSY ANIMAL, A CHILD, A CLOWN.
EVER SINCE YOU BROUGHT ME HERE
I'VE CAUSED YOU TO DESPAIR
BUT I CAN'T GIVE UP ON MY DREAM
IF YOU SAY "YES" I SWEAR—

I'LL ALWAYS FACE YOUR ENEMIES
FOR YOU I'LL BRAVE THE DEEP
FETCH YOU A PENDANT FASHIONED FROM A STAR
FOR YOU I'D FLY TILL MORNING
PROUDLY WIN A BATTLE SCAR

WHEN SOMETHING'S RIGHT YOU SEE IT FROM A FAR
AND WENDY CAN'T YOU FEEL IT?
WE JUST ARE.

During the following, **MR DARLING** *appears with his grown-up, bespectacled son,* **JOHN,** *in evening wear, at his side to observe:*

PETER

MARRY ME

WENDY

LET'S START OUR LIFE TOGETHER

PETER

MARRY ME,

WENDY

FOREVER AND A DAY.

PETER

I'M IN A SPIN ABOUT YOU
I SEE NOW THAT WITHOUT YOU
I'M A BOY
MAKE ME A MAN AND

PETER AND WENDY

MARRY ME.

MR DARLING Absolutely not! Marry this good-for-nothing? Are you out of your mind, Wendy?

JOHN I think you ought to hear them out, Pa.

MR DARLING Be quiet, John. This man has no pedigree. *(to* **PETER***)* I already have two sons who are an extreme disappointment to me. I see no reason to further sully the Darling name with another wastrel.

JOHN Father, I would hardly call my research wasteful. Why, the Society for Clinical Psychology—

MR DARLING When I want your opinion, John, I'll give it to you. *(to* **PETER***)* Young man, I forbid you to see my daughter again.

WENDY Father!

MR DARLING No, Wendy. I want a son-in-law that I can be proud of. We've had enough of this savage and his childish adventures in this house.

WENDY But he plans to grow up now. He'll change.

MR DARLING You will be ruled by me in this matter. Go to your room.

WENDY But—

MR DARLING *(bellows)* I said, go to your room!

Dogs bark.

WENDY *(reproachfully)* I wish Mother were alive!

MR DARLING So do I! John, show this chancer to the door.

WENDY *(as she goes, to* **PETER***)* I'm so sorry.

MR DARLING *(calling off)* Nana! Is this a respectable household or a zoo?!

Exit all but **MR DARLING***.*

Dogs stop.

Alone, **MR DARLING** *sings.*

SONG: "LOVING A LOST BOY - REPRISE"

LOVING A LOST CHILD'S
NOT AS EASY AS IT MAY SEEM.
LOVE HER A BIT TOO MUCH
AND SHE'LL VANISH AWAY LIKE
A SUMMER NIGHT'S DREAM.
SO WHEN SHE NEEDS YOUR LOVE
YOU JUST NEED TO FIND THE KNACK,

OF GUIDING HER FIRMLY
WHILE PRAYING
SHE'LL LOVE YOU BACK.

MR DARLING *leaves.*

End of scene

Scene Five

JOHN *and* PETER *in the hallway.*

JOHN Sorry about that, old chap.

PETER *(stunned)* The old man does not think I can be "normal".

JOHN He's got very protective of Wendy since Mother. And Michael and I became such a disappointment to him.

PETER I don't understand.

JOHN Well, you're a homeless urchin with no prospects. You must admit you're hardly a *(quoting* Hamlet*)* "consummation devoutly to be wished".

PETER When I dreamt of this, everything was perfect.

JOHN *(excited)* Did you say you've dreamt of this?

PETER Many times. Of course I didn't know the words "to marry" but I dreamt of being with Wendy forever, reuniting with you and Michael. Why is it harder than catching rabbits with a fishing rod?

JOHN I may be able to help you there. You see, dreams are something of a speciality of mine. The interpretation of dreams is a keystone to understanding our lives. In fact, I've just returned from writing a paper in Zurich with a most inspiring tutor.

PETER *(amused)* John, you're as big a swot as ever!

JOHN Honestly, this is interesting. I believe everyone who returned from Never Land is haunted by a kind of group hysteria that prevents us from leading conventional lives. If we crack its meaning, we may achieve some peace of mind.

PETER I just want to give Wendy some marry.

JOHN *(ignoring him)* Face it, none of us has been very successful adults. Wendy mopes around after you and has refused several excellent proposals of marriage – much to Father's annoyance – the Lost Boys can only keep their delinquency in check for a short while. Michael has chosen a life on the stage—

PETER "Stage"?

JOHN There you are, you see. Michael has chosen to subjugate our childhood trauma by indulging in...an "unconventional" lifestyle. I, on the other hand, felt compelled to seek absolution through the obsessive pursuit of clinical psychology. My colleagues, though divided on the exact interpretation of dreams, are all agreed that they are a manifestation of our desires and fears. Decode and confront the fear and the controlling desire can be dissipated, allowing peace of mind and liberation from our obsessions. Is this making any sense?

PETER No.

JOHN Well, let me know if you have any more vivid dreams. I may be able to unlock something. Right, you can't stay here with Father on the war path. Why don't we rejoin the delinquents, see if they can help?

End of scene

Scene Six

Backstage at the music hall.

Backstage commotion. The sound of an orchestra tuning up.

NIBS, SLIGHTLY, JOHN, MICHAEL *and* **PETER** *push through a gaggle of showgirls played by the actresses who were previously* **CISSIE, MABEL, GWENDOLYN** *and* **EDITH,** *with feathered headdresses.*

MICHAEL *is wearing a dressing gown over his stage costume. (Although we never see it.) He is little, lithe and confident. Despite what we'll learn of his history, he is not camp in our contemporary sense. However, his wit and emphatic nature differentiate him from the others.*

JOHN Backstage chaos never ceases to amaze me. It's a wonder anything get's done.

MICHAEL It amazes us too. *(to* **PETER***)* It's so good to see you again, Chief.

JOHN He needs a place to stay, Michael. 'Run-in with Father.

MICHAEL Say no more. You're welcome at ours. But are you sure you want to give it all up? Eternal youth and all that?

PETER Peter Pan has no fear of "normal". He laughs in the face of it!

MICHAEL Well, you must admit it's hard to imagine. The boy who never grew up walking down the aisle.

PETER Is the old man right? Will I make Wendy unhappy like the sea eagle crying for her lost chick?

MICHAEL Oh, don't take too much notice of Father. And I dare say Wendy's got the whole chick thing planned out.

A burst of laughter from **NIBS, SLIGHTLY** *and the chorus girls.*

Will you Lost Boys leave those chorus girls alone!

PETER *(refering to the Chorus Girls, in their feathered headdresses)* Those feathered squaws are most appealing. Should I offer them intercourse?

MICHAEL Believe it or not, it isn't obligatory. Not that you'd know it from the carryings on around here. Where's that meathead Tootles anyway?

NIBBS Joining us later, apparently.

SLIGHTLY The twins have a cold.

NIBBS Both of them.

SLIGHTLY Simultaneously.

PETER What adventures do you have in this hall of the music?

MICHAEL My partner and I perform death-defying feats on the flying trapeze.

PETER You can still fly?

MICHAEL Well, in a manner of speaking. You got me hooked.

PETER *(galvanised)* Hook?!

MICHAEL No, no. I didn't mea – it's just an expression—

SLIGHTLY May he rot in the stomach of that crocodile.

MICHAEL *(to* PETER*)* My partner and I, we dress as Red Indians. We're not top of the bill yet. They're all here to see the magic of the dark and mysterious Captain Illusion. But once that oddball moves on, I have every expectation we'll headline.

PETER You are happy here?

MICHAEL It's no Never Land but it's the right place for me. You see—

SONG: "MUSIC HALL"

WHEN I GOT BACK FROM NEVER LAND
I GOT INTO TROUBLE A LOT.

WHEN YOU'VE FLOWN ALL NIGHT
THROUGH THE BRIGHT STARLIGHT
HOW DO YOU ADAPT TO NOT?
WHY WOULD AN INDIAN BRAVE
REMEMBER HOW TO BEHAVE?
QUITE SIMPLY, I FORGOT.
SO MY TEMPER FLARED
TILL THEY TORE THEIR HAIR
AND SENT ME TO REFORMAT'RY SCHOOL.
I DESPISED IT THERE
WHERE THEY STOLE MY BEAR
AND I COULDN'T OBEY ONE RULE.
SO I'D DREAM IN BED
EV'RY TEACHER BLED,
WHEN I SCALPED HIS HEAD –

AND I FLEW OOH
TO THAT INDIAN TRIBE I KNEW.
YES, I FLEW OOH
AND WE DANCED THE WHOLE NIGHT THROUGH.
MY TRIBE AND I,
STEPPING SIDE BY SIDE,
'NEATH A STARLIT SKY,
JUST LIKE WE'D ALWAYS DO.

WHEN I CAME OF AGE I FLED THAT PLACE.
AND IT WASN'T A DAY TOO SOON.

Tune slows up.

AND I THOUGHT I'D GO
TO A CIRCUS SHOW
ONE FATEFUL AFTERNOON.

Beat.

THERE, HIGH ABOVE THE FUN,
AMAZING EVERYONE,
THERE WAS—

(spoken) An Indian!

Slow. Full of wonder.

AND HE FLEW OOH.
ON THE FLYING TRAPEZE HE FLEW.
HE FLEW OOH.
JUST LIKE I USED TO DO!
HE LOOKED MAGNIFICENT,
LIT UP THAT CIRCUS TENT,
AN ANGEL, HEAVEN SENT.

Tune speeds up again.

I KNEW FOR SURE
I WOULD BE HIS SQUAW
WHEN HE FLASHED THAT SMILE AT ME.
THAT NIGHT I DANCED
IN HIS ARMS ENTRANCED
BY MY LIVING FANTASY.
JUST SOME CIRCUS MAN
BUT IN THAT CARAVAN –
WE FLEW OOH!
MY BRAVE AND I WE FLEW!
WE FLEW OOH!
MAKING LOVE THE
SUMMER THROUGH!
TILL SOME ROUSTABOUT
MADE SURE THEY KICKED US OUT

BUT I HAD NO DOUBT –

Rhumba.

I'D ALSO LEARN THE HIGH TRAPEZE
AND FLY AS I HAD THEN.
AND WE WOULD FIND A PLACE AND TIME
WHERE MEN LOVED OTHER MEN.

THE MUSIC HA-ALL.
WHERE LOVE IS MORE INFORMAL
THE MUSIC HA-ALL
WE CELEBRATE ABNORMAL.
AND DANCING GIRLS
LOVE DANCING BOYS.

BUT IT'S A DEN
WHERE OTHER MEN
LOVE THEM AND THEN
THE GIRLS AGAIN.
WHO CARES 'CAUSE WHEN
YOU COUNT TO TEN
A COCK'S A COCK,
A HEN'S A HEN?
AND WHAT THEY'VE LAID
IS UP TO THEM.
AND THAT'S MY LIFE AS I RECALL
AND WHY I JOINED THE MUSIC HALL,
HOW I BECAME AN ACROBAT.
BUT NOW IT'S TIME THAT YOU WERE SAT.
THE CURTAIN IS ABOUT TO PART
THE MAGIC IS ABOUT TO START
YOU'LL LAUGH, YOU'LL GASP, YOU'LL CLAP YOU'LL CHEER.
I KNOW YOU'RE GONNA LOVE IT HERE!

ALL

WHERE LOVE IS MORE INFORMAL.
THE MUSIC HALL
WE CELEBRATE INFORMAL
THE MUSIC HALL
THE MUSIC HALL
THE MUSIC HALL
THE MUSIC HALL
THE MUSIC HALL
THE MUSIC HALL
THE MUSIC HALL
THE MUSIC HALL
THE MUSIC HALL
THE MUSIC HALL

Dance break.

WOMEN

AND DANCING GIRLS
LOVE DANCING BOYS.

MEN
> BUT IT'S A DEN
> WHERE OTHER MEN
> LOVE THEM—

WOMEN
> AND THEN
> THE GIRLS AGAIN.

ALL
> WHO CARES 'CAUSE WHEN
> YOU COUNT TO TEN

MEN
> A COCK'S A COCK.

WOMEN
> A HEN'S A HEN.

ALL
> AND WHAT THEY'VE LAID
> IS UP TO THEM.

MICHAEL
> AND THAT'S MY LIFE AS I RECALL,
> AND WHY I JOINED THE MUSIC HALL.

Counterpoint section.

ALL	**MICHAEL**
AND DANCING GIRLS	AND WE FLEW OOH
BUT IT'S A DEN	ON THE FLYING TRAPEZE WE FLEW
LOVE DANCING BOYS	WE FLEW OOH
WHERE OTHER MEN	JUST LIKE WE USED TO DO!
LOVE THEM AND THEN	WE LIVE HERE QUITE CONTENT
THE GIRLS AGAIN	OUR AEROBATIC BENT
WHO CARES 'CAUSE WHEN	MAKES US MAGNIFICENT.
YOU COUNT TO TEN	
A COCK'S A COCK	
A HEN'S A HEN	

AND WHAT THEY'VE LAID
IS UP TO THEM
THAT'S WHY I JOINED—

ALL
THE MUSIC HA-ALL.
THERE'S NO SUCH THING AS NORMAL.
IN MUSIC HA-ALL
WE CELEBRATE INFORMAL.
THE MUSIC HA-ALL.
THERE'S NO SUCH THING AS NORMAL.
IN MUSIC HA-ALL
WE CELEBRATE INFORMAL.
WELCOME TO THE MUSIC HALL!

WENDY *arrives.*

JOHN Wendy! Does Father know you're here?

WENDY I don't care. I've run away.

MICHAEL Wend!

WENDY *(to* **PETER***)* Don't worry about Papa. He just wants what's right for me and when he sees how happy you'll make me, he'll come round.

MICHAEL *(to* **PETER***)* You'd better make her happy because if you don't I'll set my own Geronimo on to you.

JOHN *(to* **WENDY***)* Where? When are you going to do this?

WENDY I don't know.

PETER I should like to have the ceremony of hitched under a waterfall with a choir of mermaids.

MICHAEL Well, there's that island in the middle of St James's Park and the gang here love a sing-song.

WENDY That's settled then. We'll marry there as the sun rises over Buckingham Palace and be king and queen of the dawn.

MICHAEL Oh, that's so beautiful. I think I'm going to cry.

VOICE CALL BOY Mr Darling, to the stage please. Mr Darling to the stage.

MICHAEL Oh! Show time!

PETER May we stay and watch?

MICHAEL Of course, I shall insist they give you the best seats in the house.

PETER I hope Wendy and I will be as happy as you and—

MICHAEL Geronimo. You don't... "disapprove"? Two men...

PETER Not a bit. In fact I would be honoured if you'd be my first man.

MICHAEL Pardon.

PETER My first man. At the wedding.

MICHAEL I'd love to.

JOHN You know he means "best man", right?

MICHAEL I know what he means! Now everybody take their seats before I go all unnecessary again.

End of scene

Scene Seven

The music hall auditorium.

The Company sit in a line of chairs as if in the row of an audience. They gasp in time to the music as if watching a trapeze act.

SONG: "SMOKE AND MIRRORS"

PETER *(gazing adoringly at* WENDY*)* Michael and his squaw mate! They're amazing.

All look up and gasp.

WENDY It reminds me of when we first flew. Remember when you pretended you wouldn't catch Michael?

PETER *(seriously)* I didn't plan to.

WENDY I keep drifting into a daydream of us all above the clouds. Won't you miss it?

PETER Perhaps, but I'll have you, Wendy. It was so lonely without you.

AUDIENCE MEMBERS Sssh!

The onstage audience applaud the end of MICHAEL*'s act.*

We hear the voice of the music hall CHAIRMAN.

CHAIRMAN *(offstage)* And now, Ladies and Gentlemen. The moment you have all been waiting for, the magician who's kept London spellbound with his dark art, the mysterious, intoxicating sorcery of the enigmatic, charismatic, Captain Illusion.

WENDY *is nodding off on* PETER*'s shoulder.*

PETER Wendy, wake up. You will miss the warlock!

Sinister lights and music indicate the following is **WENDY**'s *nightmare.*

Through the smoke **CAPTAIN ILLUSION/HOOK** *appears.*

Flanked by the four showgirls, his movements are brilliantly choreographed so that you never see his right hand, which is a stump (no hook until the last scene).

HOOK
SMOKE AND MIRRORS,
COLOURED LIGHTS AND PRETTY GIRLS.
THEY'RE THE TRICKS THAT
MASK A SLEIGHT OF HAND.
WHEN YOU'VE SMOKE AND MIRRORS,
LIGHTS AND PRETTY GIRLS
NO ONE SEES THE DEVILRY YOU'VE PLANNED.
SMOKE SO THICK THAT YOU COULD HIDE A CROCODILE.
PRETTY LIGHTS, REFLECTED, HIDE THE TWIST.
THROUGH MY SLEIGHT OF HAND YOU'LL
MISS THE CROCODILE
TILL THAT BEAST IS CHOMPING ON YOUR WRIST.

LOST BOYS, JOHN, PETER *and* **WENDY** *gaze out front as if watching the magician.*

WENDY *(agitated)* No, no, it can't be!

PETER Silence, beloved! Peter Pan is watching the shapeshifter.

WENDY But it's—

PETER Please fill your beautiful mouth with Turk jelly.

WENDY Turkish Delight! How many more times?!

She obviously isn't going to get through to him.

John, John!

JOHN *(trying to watch and irittated)* What?

WENDY Can't you see? It's him!

JOHN Who?

WENDY Can't you see? That magician, he's only got one hand!

JOHN Don't be silly, how could you do a magic act like that? He's got two hands.

WENDY No, he hasn't! Every time we're about to see his right hand he puts it behind his back or moves a prop or a dancing girl in front of it. He doesn't want anyone to recognise him. What's he up to?

HOOK

SEE THE PRETTY BIRDS,
SEE THE FLUFFY BUNNY!

NIBS *(pointing delightedly at the magician)* Look, a bunny rabbit!

CURLY By Jove!

WENDY Can't you see? *(to the auditorium around her)* Are you all idiots? He's only got one hand!

HOOK QUIET IN THE FOURTH ROW! This next trick's especially for the young lady with the wedding jitters. *(silkily to* **WENDY***)* Won't you join me on stage, my dear? Let's give the young lady a big round of applause.

He leads **WENDY** *into his performing area. The others clap in slow motion, adding to the dream like state.*

Look around you at these idiots, with their dull marriages and their dull little lives. Do you think that's what he really wants?

SONG: "SLEIGHT OF HAND"

THEY LOVE TO LIVE IN IGNORANCE,
UNWORLDLY AND UNWISE.
THEY GOBBLE UP MY MAGIC TRICKS
AND JUST BELIEVE THEIR EYES.
BUT I KNOW YOU CAN SEE THROUGH ANY
TRICKERY I'VE PLANNED,

I'M FOOLING THEM,
YOU DON'T FOOL ME
IT'S ALL A SLEIGHT OF HAND.

IT'S A SLEIGHT OF HAND,
A SHAM, DON'T EVER FORGET
THE FORCE THAT HE USED TO BE.
DEEP DOWN YOU KNOW I SPEAK THE TRUTH
HE'LL NEVER SUIT NORMALITY,
WE BOTH KNOW YOUR WEDDING'S DOOMED,
A LIE, THIS FARCE YOU'VE PLANNED.
YOU MIGHT PRETEND HE'S CHANGED, MY DEAR
BUT IT'S A SLEIGHT OF HAND.

IT'S A SLEIGHT OF HAND
IT'S A SLEIGHT OF HAND
DON'T FOOL YOURSELF
HE'LL EVER BE A MAN.

HOOK *and* **GIRLS**

IT'S A SLEIGHT OF HAND,
IT'S A SLEIGHT OF HAND

HOOK

ADMIT IT, GIRL,
I KNOW YOU UNDERSTAND.

DON'T THINK YOU CAN CHANGE HIM,
WE BOTH KNOW THAT CAN'T BE
HE'S SELFISH TO THE ENTH DEGREE,
QUITE LACKING EMPATHY.
CAGE HIM IN DOMESTIC BLISS
HE'LL RIP THE PLACE APART
DESTROY YOUR EQUILIBRIUM
AND BREAK YOUR LITTLE HEART

WITH A SLEIGHT OF HAND,
WITH A SLEIGHT OF HAND,
I AM THE BEST MAGICIAN
IN THE LAND
WITH A SLEIGHT OF HAND
WITH A SLEIGHT OF HAND

YOUR LITTLE SHOW
WILL BE, FORGIVE ME, PANNED!

SIT DOWN!

As she does, lights restore us to normality.

SLIGHTLY *(spoken)* That's the most amazing magic act I've ever seen.

NIBS And he never uttered a word.

PETER Spirits of the earth-mother are at work here.

HOOK

IT'S ALL – SMOKE AND MIRRORS
COLOURED LIGHTS AND PRETTY GIRLS.

End of scene

Scene Eight

In the foyer after the show.

JOHN Wendy, are you all right, you look as if you've seen a ghost?

WENDY I'm fine, fine, I just... It was very hot in there. Long day.

MICHAEL *arrives in his street clothes.*

MICHAEL Did you enjoy the show?

PETER You were amazing, little Michael.

WENDY I didn't like the magician. Gave me the creeps. Can we get out of here?

TOOTLES *arrives in uniform.*

TOOTLES Evening, savages! Lot of pretty girls here. If I'd known, I'd have dropped in before, Mikey.

MICHAEL I'm sure you'll turn lots of heads in that uniform.

JOHN Tootles! You joined the army?!

TOOTLES *(indicating PETER)* The Chief, here, trained us all to be fighters. I'm not going to turn into a milksop just because you have. *(to PETER)* Come along old boy, won't you change your mind and lead us into war? All the Lost Boys are up for it.

He produces an antiquated-looking pistol.

What do you think of this? It's my grandfather's gun – used it in the Crimean War, bit of an antique but it's still got teeth. I call it The Croc after the "you know what". Think of it, the gang back together again for one last awfully big adventure.

WENDY He has all the adventure he needs, right here. We're getting married tomorrow.

TOOTLES That settles it then. Wendy, I insist you hand him over to the Lost Boys for his final night on the town as a single man.

WENDY *(to* PETER*)* My love, please don't go. I've got a bad feeling about this.

PETER What do you mean?

WENDY Something terrible will happen if I leave you alone tonight. I know it.

PETER Wendy, don't you believe I've changed either?

WENDY Of course I do... It's just... *(pulls herself together)* Yes, of course you must go out with your old friends.

MICHAEL I'll make sure he doesn't come to any harm, Sis.

WENDY Take no notice of me, I'm just overtired, that's all.

PETER Old Lady, I'll behave, I promise.

WENDY *(anxious again)* Please be careful.

PETER *(comforting)* From dawn tomorrow, Peter Pan will never leave your side.

WENDY *(reassured)* See you tomorrow.

PETER *(kissing her)* Good night, my love.

JOHN Wendy, I'll see you home. Peter, take my wallet, I suspect you're going to need it.

Everyone wishes her good night and exits.

End of scene

Scene Nine

The street.

TOOTLES Right then, where to first?

SONG: "WE ARE THE LOST BOYS"

SLIGHTLY

WE ARE THE LOST BOYS!
WE FILL ALL PIRATE HEARTS WITH DREAD

NIBS

COME LET'S RAISE A GLASS OR TWO
OR THREE OR FOUR AND HEAD
FOR ONE LAST NIGHT OF MISCHIEF
'CAUSE WHEN THE DAWN COMES THEN
OUR LEADER'S DOOMED TO JOIN OUR RANKS,
FRUSTRATED MARRIED MEN!

TOOTLES

SO THEN CHIEF LEAD ON,
WHAT IS YOUR FINAL NIGHT TO BE?
BEFORE YOU SETTLE DOWN
TO DULL RESPECTABILITY.
A BELLY FULL OF FIRE
AND THEN SOME DRUNK DEBAUCHERY?
ONE LAST GLORIOUS
AND CAREFREE,
MESSY, DRUNKEN SPREE!

ALL BUT PETER

IT'S GONNA BE A BRILLIANT LARK.
ALL LONDON IS IN FRIGHT!
TOMORROW YOU'LL BE SPOKEN FOR,
AND IT'S YOUR WEDDING NIGHT!

HE'S GETTING LAID, HE'S GETTING LAID
HE'LL STOP BEING A BOY,
HE'S GONNA LET SOMEBODY ELSE
PLAY WITH HIS FAVOURITE TOY.

HE'S GETTING LAID, AND NONE TOO SOON
GOOD LUCK MATE, HERE'S TO YOU!
WE LOST OUR CHERRY YEARS AGO.
IT'S HIGH TIME YOU DID TOO.

Light change.

End of scene

Scene Ten

The **DARLINGS'** *house.*

JOHN *is passing through and sees his father, who is carrying a bundle of love letters.*

JOHN Can't sleep, Father?

MR DARLING I haven't slept since you mother died. Just don't see the point of dreams if they're going to be broken.

JOHN What have you got there?

MR DARLING Love letters I wrote to your mother. I like to read them over now and again to keep that dream alive.

JOHN Do you still have her replies?

MR DARLING Oh, there were no replies. Later I discovered your grandfather had hidden them from her. One day he gleefully handed them all back to me unopened. He was a spiteful man and a bully. How does it happen, John? You're blissfully a Romeo, then one day you wake up...and you're Lord Capulet.

End of scene

Scene Eleven

The **LOST BOYS**, *tired and drunk in the street.*

LOST BOYS
WHOA, WHOA, WAIT THERE!
IT'S TIME FOR HOME NOW
STOP, STOP, STOP!
IT'S FUNNY, YOU GET OLDER AND YOU JUST CAN'T SEEM TO
    TOP
THE THINGS YOU ONCE DID IN YOUR YOUTH
DOES MEM'RY SERVE US RIGHT?
DID WE REALLY DRINK AND FIGHT
AND STAY UP HALF THE NIGHT?

TOOTLES *(to* **PETER**, *who's a little woozy)* Right, better get you home, old boy. He can stay with me, Michael. Early start tomorrow. See you all for the nuptials!

Everyone says good night, leaving **TOOTLES** *and* **PETER** *alone.*

PETER Which way's your place?

TOOTLES Where do you think you're going?

PETER To bed.

TOOTLES Oh, no, you're not. Well, not your own anyway! Don't want to disappoint the wifey tomorrow night, do you? We're going to sort you out with a little dress rehearsal. Show you the "ins and outs", so you can show her! The girls I have in mind won't tell any tales. And you won't need to give them another thought once they've shown you the ropes – so to speak.

A **STREET GIRL** *approaches* **TOOTLES**.

STREET GIRL Evening, Sir, going my way?

TOOTLES Good evening, my dear. I do believe a pleasant stroll in the shrubbery might be in order. Enjoy yourself, old son.

Do us all proud. And when you're through, here's my address.
Don't wake the children, will you, or Lady Edith will have
my guts for garters.

He starts to leave with his **STREET GIRL**.

PETER The moon is behind the cloud tonight. Enemies can
sneak up on us unnoticed. Best to seek safety.

TOOTLES Nonsense, old boy. Make a night of it. You'll find the
girls on this side of Hyde Park more than obliging. Watch
your wallet though; a whore'll whip it off you in a second.

TOOTLES *and the* **STREET GIRL** *exit.*

PETER *(to himself)* Perhaps one more draft of firewater.

*A girl approaches him. She'll turn out to be a bedraggled,
adult* **TINKER BELL**.

SONG: "SLIP INTO DARKNESS"

TINKER BELL Looking for company, mister? Buy me a drink
then, mister, tell me your troubles.

PETER Be gone, bedraggled siren!

TINKER BELL Don't you recognise me?

He turns to face her.

(pathetically) "Clap your hands if you believe in fairies."

PETER Tinker Bell?!

TINKER BELL The same!

PETER *(looking at her aghast)* No, no, this – this is no same.
Are you fairy no longer?

TINKER BELL Some thugs trapped me in a glass like a cockroach
and pulled my wings off. By morning, I was a woman. I
still have a tiny fairy heart though, only big enough for one
emotion at a time. So no one wants me. I love too hard and
fight too fiercely. Nothing changes.

PETER I am changing. Tomorrow I marry Wendy and become a man. What is your heart's one emotion this night?

TINKER BELL An old one. Hatred for Wendy.

PETER You will change your heart. I command it. I love her.

TINKER BELL And I want to rip out her spleen with my pointed fairy teeth.

PETER How can I make you glad for the morrow's hitching? I know! Perhaps...

TINKER BELL What? What can you possibly say or do to stop me despising her?

PETER Tootles teaches me a man can please a woman with his body. I am yet a novice but it seems straightforward. Would you like that?

TINKER BELL Exactly what I had in mind. Come with me.

PETER Where must we go?

TINKER BELL My room, a pile of rags in the eaves of an opium den.

PETER Opium?

TINKER BELL Sometimes the smoke drifts up. Helps me forget my hatred of her.
SLIP INTO THE DARKNESS
LET YOUR SHADOW BE YOUR GUIDE,
GIVE IN TO THE NIGHT
AND RELEASE THE BEAST INSIDE.
STEAL AWAY AT MIDNIGHT
THERE'S NO MOON TO SHOW YOUR STEALTH,
STEP INTO THE DARKNESS
AND MEET YOUR REAL SELF.

WE COULD FLY TILL MORNING
BABY WE STILL CAN.
I CAN SHOW YOU MORE THEN SHE CAN
HOW TO BE A MAN.
LET THIS BODY THRILL YOU

TILL YOU WRITHE IN ECSTASY.
RIDE WITH ME INTO THE NIGHT
AND SET YOUR SPIRIT FREE.

SO WHATCHA YOU GONNA DO
YOU GONNA BE A MARRIED MAN
RESPECTABLE, DISPOSABLE
THE DREADED PETER PAN?

LOVING A LOST BOY'S
NOT SO TOUGH IF YOU HAVE A PLAN.
COME ON DON'T BE SO COY,
I'M YOUR HELEN OF TROY
I CAN SOON MAKE A BOY
A MAN.

Other **STREET GIRLS** *and clients join them join them.
The company in silhouete.*

ALL

SLIP INTO THE DARKNESS
LET YOUR SHADOW BE YOUR GUIDE.
GIVE IN TO THE NIGHT
AND RELEASE THE BEAST INSIDE.
STEAL AWAY AT MIDNIGHT
THERE'S NO MOON TO SHOW YOUR STEALTH
STEP INTO THE DARKNESS
AND MEET YOUR REAL SELF.

TINKER BELL *(with backing)*

STEP INTO THE SHADOWS
COME WITH ME
STEP INTO THE SHADOWS
COME WITH ME
STEP INTO THE SHADOWS
COME WITH ME
SLIP INTO THE DARKNESS

IT'S TIME TO BE YOURSELF!

End of scene

Scene Twelve

SONG: "THE WEDDING"

The wedding.

Lights shift and the writhing couples morph into **LOST BOYS** *and* **LOST WIVES** *joyfully gathered for the wedding.*

TINKER BELL *slips away.*

WENDY *enters, looking beautiful in her wedding dress.*

EDITH *and* **TOOTLES** *(with congregation 'aah's)*
NO MORE BAD DREAMS
IN A NEVERLAND KIND OF WEDDING.
CHASING SUN BEAMS
IN A NEVERLAND KIND OF WEDDING.
THE "EVER AFTER" THAT THEY CRAVED IS DUE,
THEIR LONELY DAYS, "IF ONLY" DAYS ARE THROUGH
YOU CAN MAKE YOUR TROUBLES VANISH, WISHES CAN COME
    TRUE,
WHEN YOU CARRY HOPE OF NEVERLAND INSIDE OF YOU.

WENDY
JUST KEEP DREAMING,
KEEP BELIEVING.
FIGHTING ONWARDS AND –
WE'LL KNOW AGAIN THE HAPPINESS
WE HAD IN NEVERLAND.

MR DARLING *arrives with* **JOHN**.

(alarmed) Father! John, you betrayed us.

JOHN No, Wendy.

MR DARLING I wanted to be here, angel. I wanted to see you happy. That's all I've ever wanted. There's been too much sadness in this family of late. If he is the husband you've chosen and you tell me he will be worthy of you, that's all the assurance I need. Please, you're my only daughter, let me give you away as a father should.

WENDY Oh, Father!

They hug.

MR DARLING And gentlemen, when you got back from Never Land, all you asked of me was to be a father and instead I sent you to an orphanage. Please allow me to make amends.

The wedding music starts.

PETER and MICHAEL move into position at the top of the aisle.

Are you ready, my dear?

WENDY Yes, Father. I'm ready.

They process up the aisle and the marriage is conducted by JOHN in dumb show until the music finishes.

CONGREGATION
JUST KEEP DREAMING,
KEEP BELIEVING
FIGHTING ONWARDS AND
WE'LL KNOW AGAIN THE HAPPINESS
WE HAD IN NEVERLAND.

JOHN *(conducting the ceremony)* We are gathered here in the sight of the Pelican house to join this Lost Boy—

WENDY *(correcting him)* Man.

PETER *(confirming)* Man.

Everyone laughs delightedly.

JOHN This man and this woman in the blessed state of matrimony—

TINKER BELL bursts in.

TINKER BELL Er, can we just skip to the bit about "does anyone know of any just impediment", because I do! This stupid marriage is a big, fat lie.

WENDY Tinker Bell!

TINKER BELL *(indicating* **PETER***)* The blushing groom spent last night with me.

SONG: "WENDY'S EXIT"

Unworldly **PETER** *has no idea of the implications of this.*

PETER Why are you interrupting the solumny? *(combo of solemnities and ceremony)*

MR DARLING *(to* **PETER***)* You had better have a good explanation for this, boy!

TOOTLES The whore is obviously quite deranged. I put him safely into a carriage myself.

EDITH There you have it. *(refering to* **TINKER BELL***)* I see no necessity to believe the word of this...thing over that of my husband.

JOHN Tink, I'm sad to see the depth to which you've sunk since Never Land.

TINKER BELL My first night here, men pulled my wings off. I grew mortal. I knew no one. I had no choice but to make a living on the streets.

MICHAEL You could have come to me.

TINKER BELL *(indicating* **PETER***)* But I knew he'd come and rescue me.

MR DARLING And disappointed, you burst in here with your pack of lies because he chose my daughter.

TINKER BELL If he's so happy with her, why did he come to me last night?

MICHAEL Tink, lying's always got you into trouble.

TINKER BELL If it's a lie, then why do I have his wallet?

JOHN *(inspecting it)* Wendy, this is my wallet. The one I lent him.

PETER What is this pirate skulduggery?

MR DARLING I think we've heard enough from you young man, it appears you are still the impetuous, spoiled child you always were.

WENDY *stars to run out.*

PETER Wendy!

WENDY

I NEVER WANT TO SEE YOUR FACE AGAIN.
UNFIT TO JOIN THE RANKS OF REAL MEN.
IMMATURE BEYOND BELIEF
A JACKAL NEVER TAMES
ALL YOU'VE DONE IS SWAP
YOUR TRICKS FOR UGLY ADULT GAMES.

I don't understand. Do wild beasts attack?

MR DARLING Wait for me, my dear.

She exits.

EDITH Tootles, do something!

TOOTLES *punches* **PETER** *in the jaw, who falls to the floor.*

TOOTLES *(under his breath)* That's for getting caught. You'll get better at it.

The wedding fades away and lights switch to the street outside the **DARLINGS'** *house.*

End of scene

Scene Thirteen

JOHN *and* MR DARLING *address* PETER *as if he were lying on the doorstep.*

MR DARLING You sicken me. The Times is full of brave young men enlisting to fight for their country—

JOHN Papa, I've told you not to listen to the warmongers.

MR DARLING Silence, John! It's your wishy-washy gullibility that persuaded me to take this urchin as a son-in-law in the first place! You and your free-thinking friends need to understand that there are some things in life that are quite simply black and white, right and wrong. *(indicating* PETER*)* That this louse should consider himself to be a man when he falls so short of the bravery we see in his contemporaries disgusts me. You too, for that matter. *(to* PETER*)* The gentleman who struck you down at the altar tells me he even offered you command of a platoon of Lost Boys, and you turned it down. You are a coward, boy. A coward, a sexual deviant and a liar! For a second time, I am forced to banish you from my house. I trust it will be the last.

PETER Yes, yes! Peter Pan agrees! If that's what it will take to prove to you, to Wendy, that I'm a man, then I will vanquish your enemies. I'll show you.

MR DARLING God help the poor wretches who serve under you.

JOHN No!

PETER John, please tell Wendy I'll write to her.

JOHN This war is wrong, it's a pointless loss of life!

PETER *(ignoring him)* I'll prove myself in battle, I swear by the spirits of Never Land.

MR DARLING *(softening slightly)* Then I shall hope for the best from you. Though I fear the worst.

PETER *(determined)* Tootles can teach me to think and talk like a man of today.

JOHN Learning the vocabulary of warmongers won't help.

PETER You'll hear great things of Peter Pan's bravery. I will prove to Wendy that I'm worthy of her.

MR DARLING *and* JOHN *move away from* PETER.

MR DARLING *(tiring)* John, I'm not a tyrant, I'm just trying to protect my daughter. Perhaps he'll understand one day. This – your pacifism...explain it to me again. I shall – I promise I'll try to listen this time.

JOHN *and* MR DARLING *exit.*

End of scene

Scene Fourteen

Lights change as **PETER** *steels himself for war.*

SONG: "ONCE MORE"

PETER

> SO IT SEEMS THE DICE ARE THROWN NOW,
> DESTINY HAS CALLED MY NAME.
> THE ROAD AHEAD MAY BE A BATTLE,
> I MUST FACE IT, JUST THE SAME.
> I WILL BRAVE THE DARKEST PERIL
> FIGHT WITH ALL THE STRENGTH I CAN
> PETER PAN WILL STAND BEFORE HER
> HAVING PROVED HE IS A MAN.

> **TOOTLES, SLIGHTLY, NIBBS** *and* **MICHAEL** *enter. He confronts the them.*

> I WILL LEAD YOU INTO WAR
> WHAT ELSE IS MANHOOD FOR?
> STRIKING OUT FOR WHAT IS RIGHT
> SACRIFICING ALL FOR YOU ONCE MORE.
> ONCE MORE.

TOOTLES *(spoken)* At last, you sound like one of us. I knew you'd come around, old chap, we're right behind you. Lost Boys! To war!

LOST BOYS

> AT LAST THE THING WE'VE WAITED FOR
> OUR BORING LIFE WILL CHANGE.
> WE'RE GOING TO FIGHT FOR ENG-ER-LAND
> ENJOY A DARING GAME.
> FOR WE WEREN'T BRED TO SIT AROUND,
> OR RUN AWAY FROM PERIL,
> WE WANT TO THRASH SOME FOREIGNERS.
> AND WIN A BLOODY MEDAL!

PETER

> I WILL LEAD YOU INTO WAR

WHAT ELSE IS MANHOOD FOR?
STRIKING OUT FOR WHAT IS RIGHT

LOST BOYS *and* **PETER**
SACRIFICING ALL FOR YOU ONCE MORE, ONCE MORE.

TOOTLES *(with backing)*
SO TONIGHT WE LEAVE FOR PARIS
TO AWAIT THE BUGLE CALL.
SUMMONING US TO THE TRENCHES

LOST BOYS
ALL FOR ONE AND ONE FOR ALL!

TOOTLES
WHEN OUR ENEMIES SURROUND US,
AS ONE DAY THEY SURELY MUST,
WHEN HE ORDERS US TO KILL,
WE'LL GRIND THEM ALL
INTO THE DUST.

LOST BOYS
YES SIR!

Key change.

The entire Company including **MR DARLING** *assemble to sing.*

ALL *(grand)*
SO IT SEEMS THE DICE ARE THROWN NOW,
DESTINY HAS CALLED OUR NAME.

WENDY	**ALL**
I CAN'T THINK OF LIFE WITHOUT HIM.	AH
I MUST BEAR IT, ALL THE SAME.	AH

ALL
TIME TO FACE THE DARKEST PERIL
FIGHT WITH ALL STRENGTH YOU CAN

TILL THE DAY THAT YOU CAN SAY
THE BOY I LOVED IS NOW A MAN.

Huge finish.

BEHOLD A MAN!

End of Act One

ACT TWO

Prologue

GEORGE *is back in the reality of the trenches,* CORPORAL BIGGS *is trying to wake him.*

CORPORAL BIGGS Sir, Sir, wake up. It's two a.m.

SERGEANT MULLINS What's the trouble, Corporal?

CORPORAL BIGGS I'm just trying to wake Captain Davies, Sarge. He wanted to take second watch.

SERGEANT MULLINS Let him sleep, I'll take second watch.

CORPORAL BIGGS Looks like he's having a bad dream, Sir.

SERGEANT MULLINS Leave him be, whatever he's dreaming can't be as bad as this.

End of scene

Scene One

The **DARLINGS'** *house.* **JOHN** *and* **PETER**.

JOHN I shouldn't be talking to you.

PETER I need to conquer my nightmares before I face the men.

JOHN *(giving in)* It's no good. I can't resist sharing this stuff. 'Love it! Let me see if I can simplify my mentor's current thinking for you.

SONG: "JUNGIAN DREAM ANALYSIS"

JUNG DISAGREES THAT THE REASON FOR DREAMS
IS TO WARN OF FUTURE EVENTS.
SUBCONSCIOUS REVELATION
IS HIS BRILLIANT EXPLANATION
FOR OUR STRANGE NIGHT-TIME PORTENTS.
FOR IN A TIME OF CRISIS OUR
DESIRES AND FEARS ARE RIPE,
AND THEY PEOPLE OUR DREAMS
WITH SOME COMMON THEMES
EACH A JUNGIAN ARCHETYPE.
THERE'S SEVEN OF THESE FIGURES,
SO YOU CAN'T AFFORD TO MISS
JOHN DARLING'S CELEBRATED GUIDE
TO JUNGIAN DREAM ANALYSIS.

ALL *(backing not* **HOOK***)*

JOHN DARLING'S CELEBRATED GUIDE
TO JUNGIAN DREAM ANALYSIS.

COLLECTIVE UNCONSCIOUSNESS
IT'S THE ONLY STATE TO BE.
WHEN YOUR DREAMS ARE GRAND
AND YOU DON'T UNDERSTAND
UNCLE JUNG CAN HOLD THE KEY.

(spoken) DREAMY!

ARCHETYPAL FIGURE NUMBER ONE!

JOHN

> THE PERSONA IN YOUR DREAM IS YOU
> AND HOW YOU FEEL TONIGHT.

ALL THAT'S CLEVER!

JOHN

> YOU COULD BE A BEGGAR, KING OR SNAKE
> BUT YOU KNOW IT'S YOU, ALRIGHT.

ALL WHOEVER!

JOHN

> IN YOUR CASE IT'S NOT ABSTRACT
> SO, YOU LOOK AND SOUND LIKE YOU
> BUT I'M PREPARED TO BET THERE IS
> A DIFFERENCE OR TWO.
> IT SEEMS THIS FANTASY OF YOURS
> IS NOT AS YOU'D FORESEE
> AND WHAT'S GONE WRONG
> AND WHY IS WHAT IS
> FASCINATING ME.

ALL

> WHEN YOUR DREAMS ARE GRAND
> AND YOU DON'T UNDERSTAND
> UNCLE JUNG CAN HOLD THE KEY.

> TWO!

JOHN

> I'M THE WISE MAN FIGURE
> IN YOUR DREAM,
> YOU SEE MY WORTH?

ALL THREE!

JOHN

> YOUR TRICKSTER FIGURE'S MICHAEL,
> WHO WILL KEEP YOU DOWN TO EARTH.

ALL FOUR!

JOHN

> THE MOTHER FIGURE REPRESENTS
> A SOURCE OF PEACE AND WEALTH,
> IT'S CLEAR IN YOUR SCENARIO
> THAT'S NEVER LAND ITSELF.

ALL

> *(beneath)* AH!

JOHN

> SO FAR, SO STRAIGHTFORWARD
> BUT THERE'S MORE WE CAN RETRIEVE.
> I'M GOING TO PSYCHOANALYSE
> THE PROBLEM I PERCEIVE.

ALL

> WHEN YOUR DREAMS ARE GRAND
> AND YOU DON'T UNDERSTAND
> UNCLE JUNG CAN HOLD THE KEY.
> FIVE!

> *A vision of* **WENDY** *appears.*

JOHN

> THE DIVINE CHILD REPRESENTS
> ALL THAT YOU HOPE FROM FUTURE LIFE
> LIVING IN CONTENTED BLISS
> WITH WENDY AS YOUR WIFE.

ALL

> SIX!

JOHN

> TINKER BELL'S YOUR AIMA
> THE FEMALE FORM OF YOU.
> CONTRASTING AND COMPARING
> GIVES A VALUABLE CLUE.

> *The vision of* **WENDY** *disappears.*

PETER

> BUT IF NO ONE WILL BELIEVE
> I'LL REACH MATURITY—?

ALL
> SEVEN!

Music slows.

JOHN
> WELL, THEN YOU MUST DEFEAT
> YOUR SHADOW,
> THAT'S JUNG'S REMEDY.

PETER *(spoken)* My Shadow?

ALL *(hushed with fear)*
> WHEN YOUR DREAMS ARE GRAND
> AND YOU DON'T UNDERSTAND
> UNCLE JUNG CAN HOLD THE KEY.

PETER *(spoken)* What's my Shadow?

JOHN
> JUNG TEACHES THAT OUR SHADOW
> IS THE THING THAT WE MOST FEAR.
> THE ISSUE WE'RE AVOIDING,
> IN A DREAM SPEAKS LOUD AND CLEAR.
> THOUGH BY DAY WE DRIVE AWAY
> THE SHADOWS FROM OUR MIND
> BY NIGHT THERE'S NO ESCAPING FROM
> WHAT OUR SUBCONSCIOUS FINDS.
> PERHAPS IT'S SOMEONE FROM OUR PAST
> OR TERROR HIDDEN DEEP
> THE MEANS BY WHICH WE CONQUER IT'S
> ENCODED IN OUR SLEEP.

ALL
> JOHN DARLING'S CELEBRATED GUIDE
> TO JUNGIAN DREAM ANALYSIS.
> COLLECTIVE UNCONSCIOUSNESS
> IT'S THE ONLY STATE TO BE.
> WHEN YOUR DREAMS ARE GRAND
> AND YOU DON'T UNDERSTAND
> UNCLE JUNG CAN HOLD THE KEY.

JOHN

DON'T BE A FREUD!

ALL

REMEMBER THIS!

JOHN

JOHN DARLING'S CELEBRATED GUIDE

ALL

TO JUNGIAN DREAM ANALYSIS!

PETER If I hadn't seen Hook swallowed whole by a crocodile, I'd guess he was my shadow.

HOOK'S VOICE *(offstage)* More Opium! Opium! You foreign devils!

JOHN Don't forget the shadow is not always a person. Sometimes the shadow is yourself.

End of scene

Scene Two

SONG: "DRAGONS"

The opium den.

HOOK'S VOICE *(offstage)* Bring me more of that infernal concoction. I can see his face again!

He stumbles in with an opium pipe. "Civilian" clothes. A bedraggled, grizzled, slightly-demented version of the magnificent figure he used to be.

HOOK

ON THE PLAYING FIELDS OF ETON
I WAS QUITE THE STAR.
NOW LOOK AT ME, WHAT MISERY,
HOW DID I FALL THIS FAR?
THE CAPTAIN OF A FRIGATE,
THE ONCE TERROR OF THE SEAS,
CURSE YOU PAN, YOU TOOK A MAN
AND BROUGHT HIM TO HIS KNEES.
OPIUM'S MY ONLY COMFORT,
TEMPORARY JOY
BLOTTING OUT THE RECOLLECTION
OF THE WRETCHED BOY.

SO I'M CHASING DRAGONS
TO BRING ME PEACE OF MIND.
DRAGONS,
IN THE DARKNESS HELP
ME LEAVE THE PAST BEHIND.
DRAGONS, IN THE SMOKE THEY GROWL
THEIR SOFT AND LOW HELLO.
AND WHEN THEY NUZZLE ME,
I CAN BE FREE OF
THE DREAMS OF
A BOY I USED TO KNOW.

LIKE SOME RAT WITHIN A WHEEL,
MY THOUGHTS KEEP TUMBLING BACK

TO HIS CROW OF TRIUMPH
AT THAT CROCODILE'S ATTACK,
HOURS I LAY WITH ITS BELLY
NOTHING BUT TO BROOD,
TILL IT SPEWED ME FORTH,
A MESS OF UNDIGESTED FOOD.
EV'RY MAN HAS HIS OBSESSIONS
BUT MINE'S NOT THE SAME,
I CANNOT SLEEP FOR MUTTERING
AND SPLUTTERING HIS NAME.

SO I'M CHASING DRAGONS
TO BRING ME PEACE OF MIND.
DRAGONS,
IN THE DARKNESS HELP
ME LEAVE THE PAST BEHIND.
DRAGONS, IN THE SMOKE THEY GROWL,
THEIR SOFT AND LOW HELLO.
AND WHEN THEY NUZZLE ME,
I CAN BE FREE OF
THE DREAM OF
A BOY I USED TO KNOW.

BREATHING DRAGON SMOKE AWHILE
OBSCURES HIS MOCKING GRIN.

PETER'S VOICE *(offstage)* "Oh the cleverness of me!"

PETER *(terrified)* No!"
HOOK
DON'T LET THE DEMON IN!

TINKER BELL *enters.*

Her hard-boiled pragmatism constantly bursting the Gothic magnificence of his misery. (How's that for a stage direction!)

TINKER BELL Sounds like those dragons have got you on the run again.

HOOK Pixie? Is it you? Pixie, tell me. Is there news of him?

TINKER BELL Don't Pixie me, you patronising old turd! Where's my wings? You promised me you'd get my wings back.

HOOK If you helped me. If you helped me destroy Peter Pan.

TINKER BELL *(maliciously)* You missed your chance. He was here. I got him for you. We spent the night together.

HOOK What?!

TINKER BELL I laughed when he stepped over you to get to me. After we'd done it five or maybe six times, I had one of my all-important changes of heart. Passion turned to anger. You see a fairy's heart, even an ex-fairy's heart, is so small it can only handle one emotion at a ti—

HOOK Yes. I get it. Move on.

TINKER BELL My heart told me if I can't have him, Wendy won't either, so I came to give you the chance to slice his head off in return for my wings. But the opium left you dead to the world, I kicked seven bales out of you, but you just lay there in your own drool. You had your chance and you blew it! Now give me back what's mine.

HOOK Do you think I'd want it to end like that? The legendary battle between good and evil anticlimaxing in a grubby freak show in a tawdry opium den. Do you think that's a fitting finale to my ten-year obsession with the pubescent psychopath who mutilated me? With a crocodile! No, my revenge, when it comes, will be on an epic scale, unimaginable bloodshed, extraordinary suffering. It will be the stuff of legend, blighting the lives of millions for decades to come. I shall be a modern-day Caligula, if you will. Hailed throughout infamy as an Edwardian Herod for the brutal efficiency of my genocide.

TINKER BELL What are you going to do? Bore everybody to death?

HOOK SILENCE! There's got to be a clue in here somewhere, a chink in the armour, an Achilles heel. Some inspiration that will spring me from the deadlock of my inconceived revenge.

TINKER BELL Can you smell cat piss in here again? I'll bloody kill that cat.

HOOK I knew he'd betray Wendy.

TINKER BELL He didn't betray anyone. The big, stupid child. He'd no idea what he was doing was wrong. Beautiful idiot.

HOOK Ah. The noble savage personified.

TINKER BELL You what?

HOOK The concept of the noble savage as explored by Jean-Jacques Rousseau in his controversial *A Discourse on the Origin and Basis of Inequality Among Men of 1754.*

TINKER BELL You really are a sad old tosser. Well, whatever you're gonna do, you'd better do it quickly. He's leaving in a few hours.

HOOK What? Leaving for where?

TINKER BELL He's leading the Lost Boys into battle.

HOOK There's a battle?

TINKER BELL There's a whole bloody war, you blinking idiot.

HOOK I have become somewhat disengaged with current affairs.

TINKER BELL You don't even have to get off your fat arse and go buy a paper. Mrs Chang stuffs them mattresses with them. *(indicating a newspaper on the floor)* Look. Look. Right here. *(She picks it up.)* Urgh, looks like somebody killed a roach with it.

HOOK *snatches the paper and begins voraciously reading it.*

As he reads he asks absentmindedly—.

HOOK So tell me. What's it like? Intimate congress with Peter Pan?

TINKER BELL Brilliant. He was amazing.

HOOK Of course he was. Why did I even bother to ask?
Ha! No. *(thinking it through)* Yes, yes, yes. No, YES. By
Beelzebub, YES!

TINKER BELL He was shy to begin with. Then...I've never known
anything like it.

HOOK It's perfect. A long, satisfying, beautiful—

TINKER BELL Now we're talking about—?

HOOK The plan! I'm still on the plan! Get your mind out of
the gutter!

TINKER BELL Right.

HOOK With my proven prowess in battle and the War Office
stuffed with old Etonians...I should be able to secure myself
a military rank of some considerable influence. Certainly
high enough to ensure Pan gets enough rope to hang himself.

TINKER BELL You know he can't hear you, right?

HOOK *(giving her money)* Go, I need a clean set of clothes,
some pomade, new boots. HURRY!

TINKER BELL I need my wings, you bastard. Give me my wings!

HOOK I hardly think you've earned them. Do you?

TINKER BELL Please, I need them, please. I'm dying.

HOOK Pixie?

TINKER BELL My heart is too small for this body. I need to
return to who I was.

HOOK What a shame, because I've no idea where those rancid
flaps of membrane are. Perhaps even now someone's scraping
them off their shoe.

TINKER BELL You lied to me. You said you'd help me. You said
you knew where they were!

HOOK My tired old member fancied a dip in some fairy skirt. More fool you for believing me. Better hope someone who still believes in fairies will save you. Except I can't think you'll be winning too many converts. You're hardly anyone's sugar plum these days.

She runs out.

SONG: *"DRAGONS – REPRISE"*

BE GONE YOU DEMONS,
NOW I'LL HAVE A PURPOSE,
COMMANDING A BATTALION OF MEN.
WITH ALL THE DASH AND FLASH WITH WHICH
I MADE MY SCHOOL MATES SCATTER.
I MATTERED THEN,
I'LL MATTER ONCE AGAIN.
THIS MURKY ISLAND'S ON THE EVE OF BATTLE,
THE POLITICIAN'S PRATTLE OF ATTACK.
AT LAST THERE'LL BE A ROLE FOR ME,
NEW FOLLOWERS EXTOLLING ME,
WATCH OUT PAN,
FOR CAPTAIN HOOK IS BACK!

THE GUNS WILL ROAR LIKE DRAGONS,
TO BRING ME PEACE OF MIND.
DRAGONS SOUNDING DEATH KNELLS
FOR THE BOY I LEFT BEHIND.
DRAGONS,
IN THE SMOKE DEVOURING
ENEMIES FOR ME,
DISMEMBERING,
REMEMBERING,
THE MAN I USED TO BE!

End of scene

Scene Three

SONG: "THE STREETS OF PARIS"

The streets of Paris.

NIBS, SLIGHTLY, MICHAEL, TOOTLES *and* **PETER** *enter in uniform.*

NIBS D'you speak French, Sir?

PETER Give me a chance, lads, I'm only just learning to speak like you. Right, pay attention, word is they'll be moving us out to join the battle at dawn tomorrow. That gives you a night to enjoy Paris!

LOST BOYS *cheer.*

NIBS
THE EIFFEL TOWER, VINO, CROISSANTS AND PRETTY GIRLS!

TOOTLES
WHILE WE WAIT FOR ORDERS, WE EXPLORE.

SLIGHTLY
COFFEE THICK AS TAR, CIGARS AND PRETTY GIRLS.

TOOTLES
BOYS, WE'RE NOT IN CAMDEN ANY MORE.

LOST BOYS
THOUGH PERHAPS IT WOULD BE FUN
TO FIGHT A BIT

MICHAEL
I MUST SAY, WE'RE LOVING GAY PAREE!

LOST BOYS
SO UNTIL THEY SEND US TO THE BATTLEFIELD,
HAVE SOME FUN

TOOTLES
WATCH OUT FOR THE VDS.

LOST BOYS *cheer and exit, leaving a tableux of* **MICHAEL** *sauntering happily through Paris.*

MICHAEL

LITTLE PASTRY SHOPS, ON PRETTY BOULEVARDS.
THE MOST ROMANTIC CITY IN THE LAND.
AFTER DARK I WALK MONTMARTRE WITH MY LOVE,
MY MAN AND I WE WANDER HAND IN HAND.
AND WHEN WAR IS OVER, HERE ON CHRISTMAS EVE,
WE WILL RUN LIKE CHILDREN THROUGH THE SNOW.
LIVE AS SQUAW AND BRAVE AMONGST THE ARTISANS,
MY MAN AND I, BIG CHIEF GERONIMO.

PETER *and the* **LOST BOYS** *in a nightclub.*

LOST BOYS

RED HEADS, BLONDES, BRUNETTES,
SO MANY PRETTY GIRLS.
FOR THE HERO ON THE BATTLE'S EVE.
COME ON, LADS,
LET'S PICK OUR SELF SOME MADEMOISELLES,
I'VE HEARD THEY
DO THINGS YOU WON'T BELIEVE!
IT'S FOUR MONTHS TILL CHRISTMAS,
WHEN WE'RE HOME AGAIN.
THAT'S A LONG TIME WAITING FOR A KISS.
SO THE PLAN'S TO FIND
A PRETTY LOCAL GIRL
FOR A FINAL SAUCY NIGHT OF BLISS.

End of scene

Scene Four

SONG: "OOH LA LA"

An MC *takes to a small stage.*

MC Welcome gentlemen, *Bienvenue Monsieurs*, to Shadowland, the nightclub where we deliver the mysteries of Paris to your very lap. Tomorrow you leave for battle, drink deep and do not be afraid. Let Mademoiselle Lilly help you forget the dawn.

> TIGER LILLY, *an exotic cabaret dancer, takes to the stage. Flanked by three cancan girls played by the actresses who were* MABLE, GWENDOLYN/TINKER BELL *and* EDITH.

TIGER LILLY

WHEN LILLY WAS A WAS A LITTLE GIRL,
UNE TIMID PETITE FILLE,
SHE WAS SO SCARED OF ANYONE
AND ANYTHING SHE'D SEE.
UNTIL SHE NOTICED BOSSY GIRLS
COULD HAVE THEIR PICK OF BOYS,
THAT'S WHEN SHE DEVELOPED
THE TECHNIQUES SHE NOW EMPLOYS.

WITH SOME OOOH LA LA
I CAN MAKE ANYBODY FORGET
TONIGHT IS THE BATTLE'S EVE.
WHO WILL BE IN LUCK TONIGHT?
HEY, TOMMY, LIKING WHAT YOU SEE?
I'VE PLEASURED POPES AND PRINCES,
AND I'VE ENTERTAINED THE TSAR.
MAYBE THIS TIME IT'S YOUR TURN
FOR LILLY'S OOH LA LA.

WITH MY OOOH LA LA,
WITH MY OOOH LA LA,
I'M KNOWN AS MISTRESS LILLY NEAR AND FAR,
WITH MY OOOH LA LA,

WITH MY OOOH LA LA,
COME RELEASE THE BEAST IN ME,
N'EST-CE PAS?

TOMORROW ON THE BATTLEFIELD
YOUR BETTERS ARE IN CHARGE.
WHY NOT PLAY THAT WAY TONIGHT,
LET LILLY BE THE GRANDE FROMAGE?
TAKING ORDERS CAN BE FUN
WHEN LILLY'S IN CAHOOTS
IN NOTHING BUT HER BIRTHDAY SUIT
AND SPECIAL BOSSY BOOTS.

ALL

WITH AN OOOH LA LA
WITH AN OOOH LA LA

TIGER LILLY

I'M KNOWN AS MISTRESS LILLY NEAR AND FAR

ALL

WITH AN OOOH LA LA
WITH AN OOOH LA LA

TIGER LILLY

COME, COME RELEASE THE BEAST IN ME,
N'EST-CE PAS?

LOST BOYS

RED HEADS, BLONDES, BRUNETTES,
SO MANY PRETTY GIRLS.
FOR THE HERO ON THE BATTLE'S EVE.
COME ON, LADS,
LET'S PICK OUR SELF SOME MADEMOISELLES,
I'VE HEARD THEY
DO THINGS YOU WON'T BELIEVE!
IT'S FOUR MONTHS TILL CHRISTMAS,
WHEN WE'RE HOME AGAIN.
THAT'S A LONG TIME WAITING FOR A KISS.
SO THE PLAN'S TO FIND
A PRETTY CANCAN GIRL

FOR A FINAL SAUCY NIGHT OF BLISS.

In counterpoint with **LILLY** *and cancan girls singing—.*

WITH AN OOOH LA LA,
WITH AN OOOH LA LA,
I'M (SHE'S) KNOWN AS MISTRESS LILLY NEAR AND FAR,
WITH AN OOOH LA LA,
WITH AN OOOH LA LA,
COME RELEASE THE BEAST IN ME (HER),
N'EST-CE PAS?

EVERYONE *(big finish)*
LET'S HAVE SOME FUN,
WATCH OUT FOR THE VDS!

TIGER LILLY
OOH LA LA!

TOOTLES *(to* **PETER***)* What's the matter, Captain? You look as miserable as a wet Sunday in Bermondsey.

PETER I think I'll get some air, it stinks in here.

TOOTLES Right, you are, Captain.

End of scene

Scene Five

PETER *in an alleyway outside meets* TIGER LILLY.

TIGER LILLY *(very French) Bonsoir, Capitaine.*

PETER *Bonsoir, Mademoiselle.* Forgive me, but you remind me of someone, long ago. *(He can't think of the French he needs.)* Umm...*parlez-vous* the English?

TIGER LILLY Perfectly, thank you. I was beginning to think you didn't recognise me? Do I look so different?

PETER *(trying to recognise her)* I...sorry...I just can't place...

TIGER LILLY Perhaps a little war paint and a feather?

PETER Tiger Lilly!

TIGER LILLY Finally.

PETER All grown up.

TIGER LILLY Aren't we all.

PETER But what are you doing here? I mean, how did you end up in Paris?

TIGER LILLY Why not? I grew tired of people seeing me as a savage, so I moved to the most sophisticated place I could think of. Mind you, the clientele here on a battle's eve are wilder then any Indian tribe on the warpath. I'm not surprised to find you here, though.

PETER Oh.

TIGER LILLY When I heard Paris was where the troops were massing, I thought "Sooner or later, he'll pass through Lilly's on his way to adventure." Never much for the pipe of peace, were you?

PETER I could have been, I wanted to be. To settle down and marry Wendy but...

TIGER LILLY What stopped you?

PETER No one believed I could do it. Be a man, I mean.

TIGER LILLY You look man enough to me. So you're here to prove you're more than just a naughty boy. I'd have thought Wendy was more intelligent than that.

PETER She is, she was... I... I made a terrible mess of things. So I'm going to lead the Lost Boys into war and prove that I can be a man.

TIGER LILLY By going into battle? That's what Wendy wants?

PETER I don't know, I hope this will make a difference. She returns my letters unopened.

TIGER LILLY Then I think you should give her address to me. She'll read what I have to say.

End of scene

Scene Six

A street in London.

JOHN *in street clothes is trying to recruit* **PASSERS-BY**
to his peace corps.

SONG: "ADVENTURE"

PETER

THIS IS MY BIG ADVENTURE,
MY AWFULLY BIG ADVENTURE,
I'VE DIVED FROM CLIFFS TO DEPTHS BELOW,
FOUGHT MANY BATTLES AND I KNOW
ADVENTURE IS JUST CHILDREN'S STUFF,
THIS FORMER LOST'S HAD ENOUGH,
I WANT A CHALLENGE AS A MAN,
TO MAKE YOU HAPPY IF I CAN,
PLEASE, I BEG YOU, LET ME TRY.
ALL I WANT'S TO LOVE YOU AS I,
ALL I WANT'S TO LOVE YOU WHILE I,
ALL I WANT'S TO LOVE YOU
'TIL I DIE!

SONG: "UNITE"

JOHN

UNITE, UNITE,
WE HAVE TO MAKE A STAND.
THE BLIGHT OF WAR'S UPON US
AND IT'S SPREADING THROUGH THE LAND!
UNITE, UNITE,
THE BLOODSHED WILL INCREASE.
UNLESS WE ALL REFUSE TO FIGHT
AND MAKE A STAND FOR PEACE.

PASSERS-BY *turn angrily on* **JOHN**.

PASSER-BY Coward!

ANOTHER Scum.

ANOTHER My brother's risking his life for cowards like you.

ANOTHER You make me sick.

ANOTHER Get out of here.

ANOTHER Coward.

Etc.

The **PASSERS-BY** *start to throw stones at him.*

TINKER BELL *appears.*

TINKER BELL John, John this way.

End of scene

Scene Seven

They duck into an alleyway.

JOHN Thank you, they would have killed me. Did you see the anger in their faces? No wonder this government is able to hoodwink the nation. It's as if they want this war.

TINKER BELL I don't know about all that.

JOHN You look terrible.

TINKER BELL I'm all eaten up inside. The punters can sense it. No one will come near me.

JOHN Your guilty conscience, perhaps.

TINKER BELL I just didn't want him to make a terrible mistake.

JOHN You wanted him for yourself.

TINKER BELL That's true. But I know now that's never going to happen. I saw the look in his eyes on that wedding morning. He loves her, alright. But it was too late, I couldn't undo the trouble I caused.

JOHN Are you expecting me to feel sorry for you?

TINKER BELL I'm fading fast thanks to a tiny fairy heart that isn't big enough for compassion. Soon I'll be nothing more than a night light flickering into darkness. I'm dying, John.

JOHN Oh, that's a dirty trick. The lowest. You'll say anything to get Peter back.

TINKER BELL I don't expect you to believe me after the revenge I took on your family. She stole him, my beautiful boy, she came out of nowhere, sewing on shadows, inventing make-believe, trading kisses. He was mine and she stole him away.

JOHN Tinker Bell, we have to put those magical, terrible days behind us. We had an enchanted childhood but it was a curse. Moving on is our only hope.

TINKER BELL Yes, yes. That's what I want, to start afresh. To use the final days I have to warn him. I know things about Hook. I've been listening to his mutterings. I know what he's planning.

JOHN At least if you're going to lie to my face, don't insult my intelligence. Captain Hook is decomposing in the belly of a crocodile.

TINKER BELL No, no. He's not. He's on his way to France. He has a plan to destroy Peter once and for all.

JOHN Go away, Tinker Bell.

TINKER BELL You're a gentle, humane man, John. Don't you believe in fairies anymore?

JOHN For heaven's sake, I'm twenty-two years old. My countrymen are plunging head first into a futile, unjust war. I've no time for children's games.

TINKER BELL But if I could just warn him. You must know where he is. Or Wendy! Wouldn't she help me? For Peter's sake.

JOHN Stop. Stop. That's enough! All you want, all you've ever wanted, is Peter to yourself. Spin your lies somewhere else.

TINKER BELL If you could just believe in me. Give me one more chance.

JOHN I pity you. That's all I can offer. My sister has suffered enough. Now leave my family alone.

End of scene

Scene Eight

Dogs bark.

The DARLINGS' *house.*

WENDY *alone, holding a letter.*

The barking fades as she sings—.

SONG: "WENDY'S SONG"

WENDY

EVERY WOMAN HAS HER SECRET PETER PAN,
A FIGURE FROM A LONG, LOST, SUMMER DAY.
AND EVERY NOW AND THEN
SHE REMEMBERS HIM AND WHEN
THINGS COULD HAVE GONE A VERY DIFFERENT WAY.
PETER PANS DON'T LINGER VERY LONG AT ALL
BUT LONG ENOUGH TO SOMETIMES FILL YOUR HEAD
WITH THE LIFE YOU MIGHT HAVE LED
IF YOU'D CHOSEN HIM INSTEAD.
AND THE SLIGHTEST LOVERS' TIFF
CAN MAKE THEM THINK "WHAT IF..."

WHAT IF I'D HELD THE STRANGER'S GLANCE?
INSTEAD I PLAYED IT SAFE AND CHOSE ANOTHER.
WHAT IF I'D SAID "WHY NOT" TO THAT DANCE?
AND THE CHANCE OF OTHER WORLDS I MIGHT DISCOVER?
WHAT IF I'D CHOSEN BETTER? WORSE?
OR SIMPLY DIFFERENTLY?
IF I ONLY HAD ANOTHER OPPORTUNITY.

SO IN OUR DARKEST HOUR, WE THINK OF PETER PAN,
HE REPRESENTS THE PATH WE DIDN'T TAKE,
HE'S THE ONE WHO HOLDS THE KEY,
TO THE GIRL WE'LL NEVER BE,
THE FACE WE'LL NEVER SEE WHEN WE AWAKE.

JOHN *enters.*

JOHN Wendy, why are there suitcases in the hall? Nana's looking at me as if it's the end of the world. What's going on?

WENDY I received a letter from Tiger Lilly. She believes Peter is truly contrite. She reminds me of what a lying, scheming, jealous little whore that fairy is.

JOHN And that's enough? That's enough to drive you back into his arms?

WENDY John, for someone who studies the human mind, you know remarkably little about love.

During this we see a tableaux of TINKER BELL'*s deterioration.*

MY TRAGEDY'S I NEVER RAN FROM PETER PAN.
THE MOMENT THAT I SAW HIM IT WAS CLEAR
I HAD NO OTHER CHOICE BUT TO MOTHER HIM, REJOICE
-ING IN THIS SMOTHERING OBSESSION
THAT HAS DRIVEN ME TO HERE.

SOMETIMES WOMEN ENVY ME MY PETER PAN.
OF COURSE. HE SEEMS A CATCH, HOW COULD THEY KNOW?
HOW I ENVY THEM THEIR LIVES,
LIVING QUIETLY AS WIVES.
AS I LEAP FROM CLIFF TO CLIFF
I TOO ASK "WHAT IF".

WHAT IF I'D MET A NORMAL MAN INSTEAD?
SOMEONE QUIET, RESPECTABLE AND BORING?
WOULD LIFE BE BETTER IF I LAY IN BED
LISTENING TO SOME NICE SCHOOLTEACHER SNORING?
WHAT IF I'D CHOSEN BETTER? WORSE?
OR SIMPLY DIFFERENTLY?
IF I ONLY HAD ANOTHER OPPORTUNITY.

SO WHILE OTHER WOMEN DREAM OF PETER PAN,
I ENVY THEM THE PATH THEY CHOSE TO FLY.
FOOLISH TINKER BELL,
WHAT YOU'RE LONGING FOR IS HELL.
BUT IF YOU SHOULD STEAL HIM, I WOULD DIE.

(*spoken*) I'm going go to France to find him. I don't expect you to join me. I know you loathe and detest the war.

JOHN As a matter of fact, it seems Dr Jung has found a way people like us, with a questioning mind and a little bravery, can play a role without adding to hostilities. We'll need a strong stomach but he writes of a Swiss organisation he supports. They are called the Red Cross, politically neutral but doing valuable work saving the lives of the wounded. He asks if I can make up a British unit.

WENDY Then that is exactly what we will do. We shall form a Kensington Gardens division to help people suffering in this awful war, and I will be reunited with my husband.

JOHN A division made up of who? The two of us are hardly a force to be reckoned with.

WENDY We shall enlist Lady Edith and the Lost Wives Club.

JOHN Still not enough.

WENDY I've got it! Who took care of us when we were young?

JOHN Well...Nana, but what's that dog got to do with anything? She's an old lady now.

WENDY But her puppies aren't. And their puppies. We shall train them to search out the wounded and lead us to their aid.

JOHN That's brilliant. Nana will be so proud.

End of scene

Scene Nine

SONG: "UNITE"

The street.

EDITH *and* **MABLE** *and* **CISSIE** *in street clothes join* **JOHN** *and* **WENDY** *and they sing—.*

THE RED CROSS CORPS
UNITE, UNITE,
YOU WOMEN OF KENSINGTON GORE!
WE'LL PREACH AND REACH AND TEACH AND THEN
UNLEASH OUR DOGS OF WAR!

This image merges with **TOOTLES, MICHAEL, NIBS** *and* **SLIGHTLY** *marching proudly as if to battle.*

ALL
UNITE, UNITE,

THE RED CROSS CORPS
CANINE, YOU AND I!
YES, WE CAN HELP THE WOUNDED MEN
TOGETHER IF WE TRY!

The sound of dogs barking fades to an echo.

End of scene

Scene Ten

The battlefield.

JOHN, WENDY *and the* **LOST WIVES** *exit.*

TOOTLES, MICHAEL, NIBS *and* **SLIGHTLY** *hold their pose and then slowly melt out of it as the horrific sounds of the battlefield fill the air.*

They sing, aghast at the horror around them.

SONG: "LOST - REPRISE"

ALL

DEAR LORD, MAKE IT STOP!
WE ARE LOST IN THE MUD.
IN THE CARNAGE, AND SCREAMING,
YOUR CHILDREN ARE DROWNING IN BLOOD.
EVERY BREATH BROKEN GLASS,
EVERY STEP IS THE LAST.
IF I STUMBLE AND FALL NOW,
DEATH WILL CATCH UP WITH ME FAST.
THE GREY'S CLOSING IN,
I AM FINISHED,
EXTINGUISHED.
IF I DIE, AT LEAST IT MEANS I'LL SLEEP—

ALL *fade away except* **MICHAEL**, *alone, bloody, traumatised.*

MICHAEL SONG: "MUSIC HALL - REPRISE"

THEY SAID WE'D STOP BY CHRISTMAS
BUT NO END SEEMS EVER IN SIGHT.
WHEN WE HEARD THEM SAY
WE'D CHARGE NEXT DAY,
WE DIDN'T SLEEP THAT NIGHT.
THAT'S WHEN GERONIMO
WOULD WHISPER SOFT AND LOW

OF THE LIFE WE'D LEAD IN A PARIS FREED
FROM THE POUNDING OF THE GUN.
WE BELIEVED IT TOO,
AND IT GOT US THROUGH,
HOW I WISH WE'D TURNED AND RUN.
MAYBE COWARDICE,
BUT INSTEAD I'D MISS
HIS FINAL KISS.

BEFORE - HE FLEW OOH,
AS THE BOMB RIPPED HIM IN TWO,
YES HE FLEW OOH,
THERE'LL BE NO CHRISTMAS TREE
FOR MY BRAVE AND ME
THIS YEAR IN OUR PAREE -

But he breaks down sobbing. He is shell-shocked.

End of scene

Scene Eleven

A shift of light takes us to the Red Cross Military Hospital. **EDITH, CISSIE** *and* **MABLE** *in filthy nurses' uniforms and hats with Red Cross armbands.*

SONG: "FIRST AID" – (*tune*: ***BEING A MAN***)

EDITH

FIRST AID TRAINING BACK AT BASE CAMP
SEEMED AMUSINGLY EXCESSIVE,
THOSE SPRAINS AND STRAINS AND OINTMENTS FOR A BURN.
NO ONE TAUGHT US WHAT YOU WHISPER
TO A BOY AS HE LIES DYING,
SCREAMING OUT WHILST COUNTLESS OTHERS WAIT THEIR
TURN.

EDITH, CISSIE *and* **MABEL**

BUT SOMEHOW IN THE HORROR
YOU JUST LEARN.
CARRY ON.

MABEL

THOUGH DROPPING FROM EXHAUSTION, WE MUST.

EDITH, CISSIE *and* **MABEL**

CARRY ON.

CISSIE

TOO TIRED TO EVEN CARE.

EDITH

AND MY SKIN, ONCE ALABASTER,
NOW IS GREY FROM THE DISASTER
EV'RYWHERE.

MABEL

DEATH IN THE AIR

CISSIE

MY MOUTH AND HAIR.

EDITH, CISSIE *and* **MABEL**

>BUT CARRY ON.

MABEL

>JUST LAST NIGHT BEFORE THE BATTLE
>A BOY WITH LONG EYELASHES
>FLIRTED WITH ME, NOW HE'S LYING WHERE HE FELL.

CISSIE

>AND THE NINTH HIGHLAND BATTALION
>WHO PLAYED BAGPIPES TO THE SUNSET
>WERE RIPPED APART AT SUNRISE BY A SHELL.

EDITH

>MAY WHOEVER WISHED THIS ON US

EDITH, CISSIE *and* **MABEL**

>BURN IN HELL.
>CARRY ON.

CISSIE

>I THOUGHT I SAW MY BROTHER

EDITH, CISSIE *and* **MABEL**

>CARRY ON.

CISSIE

>LYING MANGLED WITH THE DEAD.

MABEL

>THEY SAY MY HUSBAND'S MISSING.

EDITH

>NO TIME FOR REMINISCING
>MORE ARRIVE.
>BARELY ALIVE.

EDITH, CISSIE *and* **MABEL**

>WE CARRY ON.

>**WENDY,** *also in a filthy nurses' uniform, enters with a wounded, bedragled* **NIBS, MICHAEL** *and* **SLIGHTLY.**

TOOTLES *bustles through in charge.*

WENDY Tootles, I need to speak to Peter.

TOOTLES Lieutenant Tooteridge, if you please. And I'm afraid Captain Pan is still unavailable.

WENDY You've been saying that ever since I arrived. Have you even told him I'm here? I demand you take him my message.

TOOTLES Steady on, old girl, war on and all that sort of thing.

EDITH Don't waste your breath, Wendy, once my husband's got an idea in his thick head. There's no shifting it. *(to* **TOOTLES***)*

She bustles off.

TOOTLES *(calling after her)* Now, Edith, don't be like that.

WENDY Do you know who you remind me of with your dogged self-importance?

TOOTLES Achiles? Ajax?

WENDY The late unlamented Mr Smee.

TOOTLES Oh, that's a low blow, Wendy. I'd like to help you gals but the Chief's got his hands full. He's to meet the big cheese for a special commendation this evening. Besides, I'd have thought you'd have enough to worry about here, Nurse Darling.

EDITH *leads a sick young woman in.*

SONG: "BELL'S STORY – REPRISE"

EDITH Casualty coming through. Young woman. Make way there. She's very weak.

WENDY Oh, you poor dear. Sit down. Let me take a look at you. *Parlez-vous Anglais?*

We and **WENDY** *see it's* **TINKER BELL***.*

You?!

TINKER BELL Wendy, please, please, you have to help me. Peter's in great danger. I must speak to him.

WENDY Do you expect me to fall for that? You're a parasite. You always have been and you always will be. Well, you won't cause any more trouble. I'll see to that. Now give this slip to the desk sergeant and he'll give you some soup. Plenty of your kind are left high and dry when the troops move on.

TINKER BELL Don't be cruel.

WENDY Don't be cruel? I barely knew the meaning of the word before I met you. You cast me as your enemy before we'd even spoken. You tricked the Lost Boys into shooting me dead before I even landed in Never Land. It was only Peter's kiss that saved me.

TINKER BELL It was an acorn.

WENDY To us it was a kiss. And it was for all time, that's why Tootles' arrow glanced off it and that's why I'm asking you to leave us alone.

TOOTLES and **JOHN** *enter separately.* **JOHN** *is in uniform now with a Red Cross armband and a doctor's bag.*

TOOTLES Alright, lads, try and get some sleep. Commander Pan may want to charge again at dawn.

JOHN No! Has he lost his reason? Wasn't today's carnage enough?

MICHAEL No! No, I can't! I can't go back. Don't make me go back.

TOOTLES Settle down there, Soldier. Nurse Darling, assistance needed here.

MICHAEL *is sobbing.*

WENDY *comforts* **MICHAEL.**

WENDY There, there, come on. *(noticing)* You're bleeding. *(calling)* Write a request for more medical supplies, and send one of the dogs with it. They'll get through quicker.

MICHAEL I can't go back, Wend.

WENDY There, there. Everything will be alright.

MICHAEL But I can't. All the noise, the smoke, the screams.

WENDY I know, I know.

MICHAEL Nothing, no nightmare ever prepared me for this. And it's all because of him! I've seen him with the other officers, sending us into the barbed wire as if we were chess pieces. Have you met up with him yet? Get him to stop this.

WENDY No, Lieutenant Tooteridge here insists he's too busy and won't let me or my messages through.

MICHAEL *(of* **PETER***)* I hate Peter.

TOOTLES Careful, Soldier. I could have you court-martialled for less.

He exits.

MICHAEL Tell us all a story, Wendy. Like you used to.

WENDY I'm too busy for happy endings tonight.

TINKER BELL I'll tell you a story.

WENDY I think we can do without your kind of stories.

TINKER BELL One of yours then, from long ago.

WENDY You always stuffed moss in your ears and said they were stupid.

TINKER BELL But I listened. And I remember every word.
THERE WAS YOU
AND THERE WAS ME, LEFT
ON THE OUTSIDE LOOKING IN.
HOW I LONGED TO JOIN THE PARTY BUT
I WAS TOO IN LOVE WITH HIM.
YOU WERE THE CONNIVING PRINCESS
LEAVING SLIPPERS MADE OF GLASS,
HE WAS MINE, YOU TOOK HIM FROM ME.
AND I NEVER STOOD A CHANCE.

YES, I KNOW NOW I WAS WRONG
BUT WHO CAN TAME THEIR HEART?
IF I KNEW THEN WHAT I KNOW NOW
MAYBE WE'D BE FRIEND'S HE COULDN'T PART
BACK AT THE START.

LISTEN, IF YOU WANT A STORY,
INSPIRATION TO GO ON,
REMEMBER HOW I LET A HATRED
RULE MY LIFE, SOON I'LL BE GONE.
THERE'S A CHANCE YOU'LL SEE TOMORROW,
DON'T THROW IT AWAY IN SPITE,
DON'T END UP LIKE ME,
A SHADOW FADING FAST INTO THE NIGHT.

WENDY Peter is in danger you say.

TINKER BELL Do you believe me now?

WENDY I...I don't know.

TINKER BELL Say it. Do you believe in me?

WENDY I... Give me time to think.

TINKER BELL After all I've done? You're the only woman who would.

WENDY Yes, but only I know the pain of loving him. I will take you to Peter.

EDITH I'm afraid it's too late. There's no heartbeat.

WENDY *(deep breath, then)* Will someone tell Lieutenant Tooteridge that I am going to talk to Captain Pan. Now!

EDITH Don't you worry about Tootles, Wendy. I'll take care of him.

End of scene

Scene Twelve

The officers' quarters. **PETER** *alone.*

PETER

WITH THE DAWN THIS MORNING
I ORDERED THE ATTACK,
MY MERRY BAND OF OUTLAWS
NEVER FALTERED OR LOOKED BACK.
MY SHADOW DANCED REJOICING
IN THE CLEVERNESS OF ME,
RECOVERING,
DISCOVERING
THE MAN I NEED TO BE.

TOOTLES *enters.*

TOOTLES Captain, we have to get you a costume.

PETER What do you mean?

TOOTLES The officers' mess is having a bit of a fancy dress party. Take everyone's mind off the latest casualty figures.

PETER Good idea.

TOOTLES All very "make do and mend" of course, but the 18th have got themselves up as cavaliers, very droll. The Field Marshall himself is putting in an appearance and is already in costume, so you'd better look sharp. He's dropping by to commend you personally, before the party.

PETER So he should. I led the men bravely and brilliantly today and more than justified his faith in promoting me so fast. I hope Wendy reads about it back in London.

TOOTLES Wendy isn't in London. She's here with that slutty fairy, Sir. Tending for the wounded with the Red Cross. Them, John and half of Battersea Dogs Home.

PETER What! Why hasn't she been to see me?

TOOTLES The Field Marshall thought it unwise, Sir. Too much of a distraction. I've strict orders that you're not to be bothered but...well, she's getting very persistent.

HOOK, *in full pirate regalia, emerges. The hand with the* **HOOK** *is in his jacket, Nelson-style, to be revealed later.*

PETER Send her to me at – *(seeing* **HOOK***)* Oh, very good, Sir. Very good, an excellent costume. Charles the First?

HOOK *(to* **TOOTLES***)* Leave us!

SONG: "WHAT ABOUT ME AND YOU?" – *(Sinister Vaudeville Style)*

TOOTLES *exits.*

What a laugh, what a laugh.

PETER What's so funny, Sir?

HOOK Do you know how much ground you captured today? Nothing! All those husbands, fathers, brothers, sons lost their lives and for nothing... It's not like the old days, is it? Being a grown-up...all very different isn't it? In the real world, plunging unthinking into peril often has consequences. In this case, very terrible consequences. In this instance, the lives of twenty thousand men. For nothing.

PETER I'm...I'm an idiot...

HOOK No, no, you're one of us. I fast-tracked your promotion, remember. Over and over again. "The Peter Pan I know will never shirk from recklessly driving his men into the abyss." I thought. And I was right. I trust you enjoyed the "awfully big adventure".

PETER I'm a monster.

HOOK Not yet, but learn to shrug this off, get back into the saddle and you could be.
YOU'VE GOT WHAT IT TAKES,
YOU LEAD WITH THE ACE,
YOU FOLLOW THE HUNCHES.

I'M A SMART KIND OF GUY,
NOT STRAIGHT AS A DIE,
BUT I ROLL WITH THE PUNCHES.
INDEPENDENTLY YOU'RE GREEN,
TOGETHER WE'RE A WINNING TEAM.
IT'S TRUE, COME ON NOW, THINK IT THROUGH,
WHAT ABOUT ME AND YOU?

He holds out his hand to PETER, *which is of course a hook.*

Come on, my boy, shake your old mate by the hook. Today's slaughterhouse was nothing. By the time we're through, this war will be the biggest bloodbath since Genghis Khan hacked half the continent to steak tartare. Unimaginable horror. I know you, boy. You never could resist a good scrap. Join the fun!

PETER *(stunned)* I sent twenty thousand men to their death.

HOOK And that's just our side! Isn't it fun?! And you're going to do it all again tomorrow!

HOOK *puts his arm around* PETER's *shoulder.* PETER *is still stunned by the casualty figures.*

WHAT ABOUT ME AND YOU?
LET ME BE YOUR DAD,
WON'T YOU COME TO SEE ME AS A FATHER?
THE CONTRETEMPS WE'VE HAD
DON'T DETER ME, I SHALL MISS THEM RATHER.
THOUGH YOU WERE UNDOUBTEDLY
A VICIOUS LITTLE BRAT,
A BULLY, CROOK AND MURDERER,
I NEED A KID LIKE THAT.

PETER France is knee-deep in corpses tonight and all because of me?

HOOK Oh, come off it. Don't pretend you have a conscience.
I CAN BE YOUR GUIDE.

HELP APPLY THE SIDE OF YOU THAT SNIGGERED
AS YOU STOOD AND WATCHED, WHEN I
BY CROCODILE WAS SO DISFIGURED.
AS I FLED THOSE JAWS OF DEATH
I THOUGHT "THAT LITTLE LAD
COULD BE A STAR, HE COULD GO FAR,
IF HE COULD CALL ME DAD."

LET ME FINISH.

KIDNAPPING AND FRAUD,
SENDING ALL YOUR LITTLE COMRADES BARMY,
ARE TRAITS THAT WE APPLAUD
IN INDUSTRY, THE LAW AND BRITISH ARMY.
YOUR FIRST DAY AS AN OFFICER
WAS TERRIBLE, ALL RIGHT.
BUT WE'VE A WAR TO WIN
SO JUST CHUCK UP, BUCK UP AND FIGHT.

JOHN, MICHAEL *and* **WENDY** *enter.*

JOHN I hope we're not interrupting anything important.

PETER Wendy?!

HOOK What's the meaning of this? How did you riff-raff get in?

TOOTLES *runs in.*

TOOTLES *(adjusting his uniform)* I'm sorry, Sir, I was distracted.

EDITH *enters in equal disarray.*

HOOK Distracted! A good soldier is never distracted.

EDITH I was distracting my husband.

HOOK Oh, I see. *(to* **TOOTLES***)* Don't blame you. Pretty little filly. *(silkily to* **EDITH***)* Good evening, my dear. *(to* **TOOTLES** *sharply)* But don't let it happen again.

WENDY *(to* **HOOK***)* Excuse me, Field Marshall. *(to* **PETER***)* We have something to say to the young Captain here.

HOOK Can't this wait?

WENDY (*sharply to* **HOOK**) Quiet!

TOOTLES (*correcting* **WENDY**) Nurse Darling! –

PETER *holds up his hand to silence him.*

PETER Wendy? Am I a man now? Is this what you wanted? All of this? Is that why you followed me here?

WENDY No. No. Never in a million years.

PETER Then please. I beg you. Tell me. What do I do? How do I do it? If not all this, how do I prove to you that I'm a man?!

SONG: "BEING A MAN – REPRISE"

WENDY

> I CAN'T ANSWER WHAT A MAN IS.
> ALL I KNOW'S I LOVED A BOY
> WHO WAS SOMETIMES CRUEL AND HARSH BUT
> UNLIKE YOU HE BROUGHT US JOY.
> HE WOULD FIGHT BUT HE WOULD NEVER
> HARM THE FRIENDS WHO CARED FOR HIM,
> YOU WOULD REALLY BE A MAN
> IF YOU GREW UP
> TO BE LIKE HIM.

PETER *and* **HOOK** *remain locked in each others stare.*

COMPANY

> NEVERLAND IS A PART OF US, STILL JUST BEYOND A STAR,
> THOUGH WE'VE GROWN TO ADULTHOOD
> IT MADE US WHO WE ARE
> DEEP WITHIN OUR HEART'S
> A SECRET NO ONE NEEDS TO KNOW
> WE STILL REMEMBER
> THAT DECEMBER
> OF MAGIC LONG AGO.

WENDY

> SEE THE WORLD AS PETER PAN DID.
> HE WOULD ALWAYS QUESTION "WHY".

DARE TO DO WHAT NO ONE ELSE DID,
HE WOULD REACH TO TOUCH THE SKY.
NEVER EATEN UP WITH ANGER,
NOT LIKE YOU, SO COLD AND GRIM.
YOU WOULD REALLY BE A MAN
IF YOU GREW UP
TO BE LIKE HIM.

HOOK William Wordsworth? "The Child is the father of the Man"? Please! That's sentimental hogwash! Let's bring it home, girls.

Incongruously, showgirl pirates tap-dance on and flank him for a big finish.

THE INFANTRY WE SENT
ARE MOSTLY DEAD OR DYING, CATASTROPHIC.
BUT DON'T GIVE IN TO SENTIMENT,
BOTH OF US ARE BORDERLINE PSYCHOTIC.
OUR WOUNDED CAN FIGHT ON AGAIN,
YOU'LL WIN, MY SON, YOU'LL SEE,
YOUR ACUMEN
FOR KILLING MEN
REMIND ME, KID, OF ME.

WENDY No! He's not like you. *(handing him a gun)* Take this and end it once and for all.

TOOTLES *(recognising his gun)* That's The Croc! How did you get hold of my gun? *(to* **EDITH***)* You conniving little bitch!

WENDY Thank you again, Lady Edith.

EDITH My pleasure, Wendy.

TOOTLES *exits.*

PETER *is aiming the gun at* **HOOK***.*

HOOK Now, boy, you wouldn't shoot an old sparring partner, would you?

PETER *shoots* **HOOK***.*

(triumphantly) That's my boy! You always were a little shit. This war's all yours now. You'll make a bigger slaughterhouse of it than I ever could. Take it away.

He staggers into a surreal kick line of the wounded **NIBS, SLIGHTLY, MICHAEL** *and Pirate Showgirls for a big finish lit in sickening, ominous colours.*

HOOK, NIBS, SLIGHTLY, MICHAEL *and* **PIRATE SHOWGIRLS**
YOU'VE GOT WHAT IT TAKES,
YOU LEAD WITH THE ACE,
YOU FOLLOW THE HUNCHES.
I'M A SMART KIND OF GUY,
NOT STRAIGHT AS A DIE,
BUT I ROLL WITH THE PUNCHES.
INDEPENDENTLY YOU'RE GREEN,
TOGETHER WE'RE A WINNING TEAM.
IT'S TRUE, COME ON NOW, THINK IT THROUGH.
WHAT ABOUT ME AND—

PETER *shoots him again. This time* **HOOK** *falls to the floor.*

The wounded men from the kick line sink back and the pirate showgirls fade off.

PETER Death to all pirates! Wendy, I don't like this adventure. We're going home. You too, Tootles, Michael, John, we're all going home.

JOHN No, Captain Llewellyn Davies, it's time to wake up now. Time to wake up. And be a man.

SONG: "ACT TWO FINALE (LAGOON - REPRISE)"

PETER We can't go back to Never Land?

MICHAEL Not yet.

PETER Will you ever marry me?

WENDY Oh yes, I'll be there. Every night. In your dreams.

End of scene

Scene Thirteen

The dream dissolves and GEORGE *is back in the reality of the trenches.*

SERGEANT MULLINS Captain Davies? Time to wake up now.

GEORGE Wha – what time is it?

SERGEANT MULLINS Four a.m., Sir.

GEORGE *(pulling himself together)* Right, right. Get everyone at the ready. We're pushing on towards enemy lines.

SERGEANT MULLINS There's reports of bombardment coming from that direction, Sir.

GEORGE Are you contradicting me, Sergeant?

SERGEANT MULLINS No, no. Of course not, Sir.

GEORGE I will have discipline under my command.

SERGEANT MULLINS Yes, Sir. But—

GEORGE But what? We have our orders, Sergeant. You're not afraid are you?

SERGEANT MULLINS A little, Sir. We all are.

GEORGE I need men, not a bunch of fairies.

SERGEANT MULLINS *runs out.*

WENDY *appears and sings—.*

WENDY *(gently)*
JUST SEE THE BLUE,
A BLUE YOU KNEW LONG AGO.
A BLUE LAGOON,
BENEATH THOSE CLOUDLESS SKIES.
IT FELT SO GRAND,
TO STAND, THAT SUN IN YOUR EYES,
THEN RACE EACH OTHER OUT

ACROSS THE SAND,
YOU'D FLY.

GEORGE I can't do it, Wendy. I can't turn back. Even for you.
I can't disobey orders. I'd be court-martialled, disgraced.

TINKER BELL *appears.*

TINKER BELL	**CHORUS**
CLIMB HIGH TO DIVE	OOH

TINKER BELL *and* **MICHAEL**
INTO THE TURQUOISE
  BELOW

TINKER BELL, MICHAEL *and*
JOHN

THE WATER WARM,	OOH

THE MERMAIDS' SONG
  SUBLIME.

ALL

REACH FOR THE BLUE,
MAYBE THOSE SUMMERS
ARE GONE.
BUT BATHE IN BRILLIANT BLUE
ONE FINAL TIME.

The other characters slowly join in beautiful harmonies.

The grey sky burns blue again.

SO LOOK AGAIN.
YOU CAN MAKE EVERYTHING NEW.
IF YOU JUST LOOK
THE WAY THAT YOU USED TO SEE.
DON'T CHOOSE THE GREY, THE DARK,
THE RATS AND THE RAIN,
JUST LOOK AGAIN
A DREAM CAN SET YOU FREE.

J. M. BARRIE *enters, watching on.*

GEORGE   *(calls)* Sergeant! Call a retreat. To hell with the consequences. We're going back. It's just...it's just The Right Thing to Do.

They turn and freeze, except **J. M. BARRIE.**

J. M. BARRIE   Dogs were regularly used in the trenches to carry messages and search for the wounded.

The Swiss psychiatrist Karl Jung did much to promote the work of the Red Cross during the First World War and his success helping the victims of shell-shock brought credibility to his analysis of dreams.

Captain George Llewellyn Davies, my adopted son, was killed in Flanders in 1915, leading his men to safety. Legend has it that he died with a copy of *Peter Pan* in his pocket.

Music swells.

The End

SONG: "BOWS"

COMPANY

> SO IT MEANS THE DICE ARE THROWN NOW,
> DESTINY HAS CALLED OUR NAME
> THE ROAD AHEAD MAY BE A BATTLE
> WE MUST FACE IT JUST THE SAME.
> TIME TO FACE THE DARKEST PERIL,
> FIGHT WITH ALL THE STRENGTH YOU CAN,
> 'TIL THE DAY THAT YOU CAN SAY
> THE BOY I LOVED IS NOW A MAN.
> BEHOLD, A MAN!

PROPS/LIGHTNING/SOUND EFFECTS

ACT I

PROPS
Antiquated-looking pistol (p43)
Bundle of love letters (P47)

LIGHTING
Darkness (p1)
Sinister lights (p38)
Lights restore us to normality (p42)
Light change (p46)
Lights shift (p52)
Lights switch to the street outside the Darling's house (p56)
Lights change (p59)

SOUND/EFFECTS
Sound of a bird singing (p6)
The sound of dogs barking (p23)
The sound of dogs stop (p23)
Dogs bark (p23)
Dogs bark (p26)
Dogs stop (p26)
The sound of an orchestra tuning up (p30)
We hear the voice of the music hall Chairman (p38)
Sinister lights and music indicates the following is Wendy's
    nightmare (p38)
The wedding music starts (p53)

ACT II

PROPS
Opium pipe (p68)
Newspaper (p71)
Money (p72)
Stones (p81)
Letter (p84)
Doctor's bag (p93)
Gun (p101)

LIGHTING
A shift of the light (p90)

SOUND/EFFECTS
Dogs bark (p84)
The barking fades as she sings (p84)
The sound of dogs barking fades to an echo (p87)
The horrific sounds of the battlefield fill the air (p88)

THIS
IS
NOT
THE
END

9 780573 115165